Chess
for Children
Activity Book

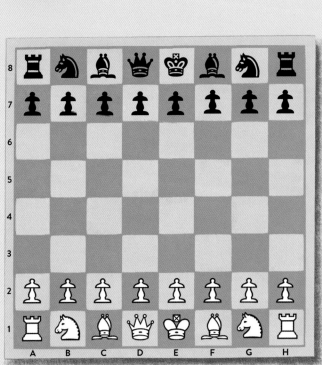

Chess for Children

Activity Book

Sabrina Chevannes

BATSFORD

First published in the United Kingdom in 2013

This reillustrated edition first published in the United Kingdom in 2025 by

Batsford
43 Great Ormond Street
London
WC1N 3HZ

An imprint of B. T. Batsford Holdings Limited

Copyright © B.T. Batsford Ltd 2025
Text copyright © Sabrina Chevannes 2013

ISBN 9781849949026

A CIP catalogue record for this book is available from the British Library.

10 9 8 7 6 5 4 3 2 1

Reproduction by Rival Colour Ltd, UK
Printed and bound by Toppan Leefung Printing International Ltd, China
Illustrations by Naomi Wilkinson

Contents

Introduction.................... 6

Revision Time: The Pawn.................. 8

Pawn Wars Strategy......................... 12

Revision Time: Rooks, Bishops and Queens.............................16

Cops and Robbers Strategy.............18

Revision Time: Knights.....................20

Hungry Horse Strategy.................. 22

A Knight's Tour 24

Chess Variants............................. 26

Jesön Mor.................................. 28

Revision Time: The King..................30

Mine Alert.............................. 32

Introduction to Strategy................34

Strategize: Knights vs. Bishops........ 36

Revision Time: Chess Notation.......40

Co-ordinate Bingo..........................44

Revision Time: Check and
Checkmate.................................48

Checkmate Challenge.....................50

Puzzle Time: Mate in One............. 52

Three Check Chess......................... 54

Thinking Ahead.................................. 56

Puzzle Time: Mate in Two................ 58

Progressive Chess...........................60

Revision Time: Scoring Points......... 62

Chess Maths...................................64

Good Capture/Bad Capture?...........66

Giveaway Chess............................. 68

Strategize: Opening Principles........70

Puzzle Time: Yes, No or Maybe....... 74

Revision Time: Pins, Forks and
Skewers...................................... 76

SPAF..80

Revision Time: More Tactics............ 82

Spot the Tactic................................86

Spot the Threat, Stop the Threat.....88

Walking the Dog Challenge.............90

Shadow Mate Challenge.................. 92

Box 'em in Challenge.......................94

Game Time: Guess the Move......... 96

Bughouse...................................... 106

Goodbye.. 109

Glossary.. 110

Index.. 114

Answers to Puzzles........................... 116

Introduction

Jess: Hey, Jamie!

Jamie: Hey, Jess! It's been a while!

Jess: I know! I haven't seen you since we worked on our first book. How have you been?

Jamie: Great, thanks! I have been practising lots of chess and I think that I am even better at it now!

Jess: Yeah, me too. I really think that practice does make perfect.

Jamie: Especially with chess – there is a lot of pattern recognition involved.

Jess: Well, this is why I called you, Jamie. I would like to do some more chess training together in the form of fun puzzles.

Jess

Jamie: Oooh, that sounds like a great idea! I know so many fun games to help us get better at chess.

Jess: I know quite a few too, and I thought I'd invite our friends Marnie and Harry along too so we could all have fun playing together.

Let's put our ideas together and make a Chess Activity Book for everyone to join in and have fun with us!

Jamie: Great idea... let's get to work!

Jamie

REVISION TIME:
The Pawn

Jamie: Since it has been a long time, I think we need to do a little bit of revision on everything we learned in our first book.

Jess: Well, I have been practicing a lot, so I think I remember everything, but it can't hurt to look over things again.

Jamie: Let's start with the pawn!

Jess: Ah yes, these little guys are deceivingly complicated. Even though they are small, they do so many confusing things!

Jamie: Yes, they are the only pieces that move differently from the way they capture.

Jess: They move forwards, but capture diagonally, right?

Jamie: Yes, they only ever move one square forwards unless they are on their starting square, when they have the option of moving two squares forwards if they want to.

You see, the pawns highlighted in green can still move two squares as they have not yet been moved. The ones in red cannot move at all as they are blocked. The others can all move, but they can only move one square as they have already been moved.

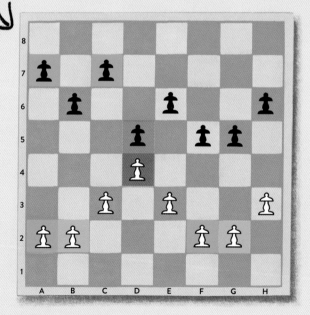

Jess: I always move mine two squares if I am allowed to. Why would you only move one square?! Surely you want to advance as much as possible?

Jamie: Not necessarily... what if someone can capture you if you move two squares?

Jess: Oh yeah, that's true. So that is why we get the option of moving one or two – it depends which is safer!

Jamie: Well, they may both be safe, but it means we have extra choices. I suppose it is to compensate for the fact that the pawn cannot move backwards.

Jess: Oh yeah, that is really annoying. I always have to think very carefully before I move a pawn, because I can't move it back if it is a mistake.

Jamie: Exactly!

Jess: Then I have to take care when the pawns are diagonally next to each other, because they can take each other. It's confusing as I just got used to them moving forwards.

Jamie: And with so many of them on the board, there are probably captures everywhere! Look at all the captures that White can make in this position! There are seven different captures to choose from!

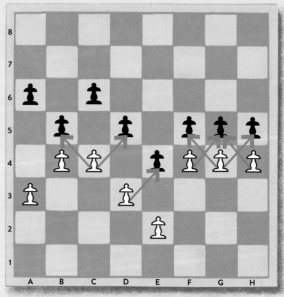

Jess: Yes, but if White can capture Black, then Black can capture White too! This position is crazy!

Jamie: Good point!

Jess: Don't you remember we talked about Pawn Magic in our first book too? The pawn did some really cool extra stuff.

Jamie: Yeah, there were two extra special moves that the pawn made – **promotion** and **en passant**.

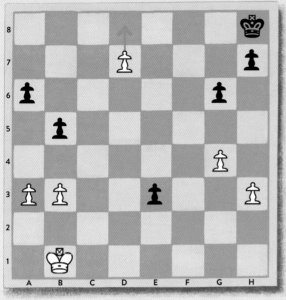

Jess: The promotion one was easy: if a pawn got to the end of the board, it could turn into a piece of its choice.

Jamie: That's right. Well, anything except a king!

Jess: Or another pawn!

Jamie: Yeah, that would be silly if it just stayed as itself and couldn't move anywhere considering it can't move backwards!

Jess: What a waste of a promotion that would be!

Jamie: I would always choose a queen because it is the most valuable.

Jess: Me too... I love the queen!

Jamie: What about en passant though, Jess? Do you not remember that one?

Jess: I do, but sometimes I get confused. I swear I have played people and they have just cheated and said it's en passant! So I am not sure what is right anymore!

Jamie: Oh, Jess! You can't let people do that to you! You were the one who taught me last time and now you have gotten all confused yourself.

Jess: I know.

Jamie: It's OK – I will explain it again. There are three main rules you need to remember about en passant:

1. Your pawn must be on its 5th **rank**, which is just past the halfway mark.

2. The pawn that you are to capture must be on the **file** next to that of your pawn and move from its starting square two squares, so that it sits next to your pawn.

3. You could then capture the pawn as if it only moved one square.

Jess: I thought that is what you do, but it is still confusing!

Jamie: Look!

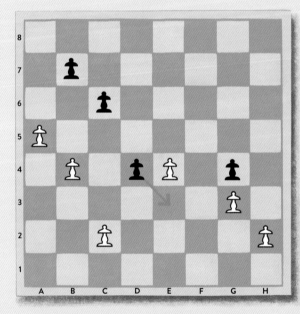

If it is Black's move in this position and White has just pushed their pawn to e4, then Black can actually capture it!

Jess: Oh yes, because the black pawn on d4 is on its 5th rank and the white pawn is on the adjacent file having just moved two squares next to it.

Jamie: What if it only moved one square?

Jess: Then it wouldn't be allowed to take it en passant, it would just capture it normally.

Jamie: Very good. The black pawn would end up on e3 and the white pawn would disappear from the board.

Jess: Here's a question for you, Jamie – if Black decided not to do that and instead decided to push their pawn to b5, what do you think White would do?

Jamie: I know what you want me to say! White can take the black pawn by en passant if that happens! However, White doesn't actually need to do that because they can just push the pawn to a6 and still win!

Jess: OK, smarty pants, but en passant is still possible there.

Jamie: Indeed it is. En passant is not compulsory, but in this case, it is definitely worth Black taking the e4 pawn!

Jess: I think I need to put these things into practice!

Jamie: Game of Pawn Wars?

Jess: Bring it on!

Pawn Wars Strategy

Jamie: We have played so many games of Pawn Wars and we beat each other all the time, but do you really know what you are doing?

Jess: Well, I do have a plan most of the time and I've developed a few cool ideas.

Jamie: Me too! Want to share?

Jess: Hmmm, I'm not sure, because then you may beat me!

Jamie: Just because I know some of your plans, doesn't mean that I can stop them all!

Jess: That's true. Plus, I'm going to keep a few of them a secret anyway.

Jamie: Fair enough. So what tricks have you got?

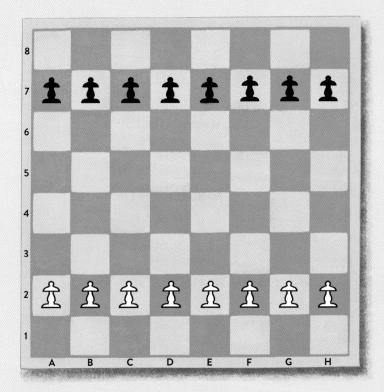

Jess: OK, so we only have pawns, right? Since they don't move backwards, I want to gain as much space as I can with them so generally I move them two squares forwards at a time whenever I can.

Jamie: But which pawns?

Jess: Well, I start with the centre pawns because controlling the centre of the board is a good idea.

Jamie: I do that too, but I don't move the pawns two squares all the time. Sometimes it is unsafe, so I prepare a double push by pushing the pawn next to it one square.

Jess: What do you mean?

Jamie: Look: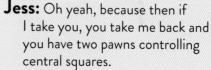

I want to push my pawn to f4, but if I do, the black pawn on e5 will just capture it for free, which is not good! So, if I push my pawn to g3 first, I can then push my pawn to f4 on the next go.

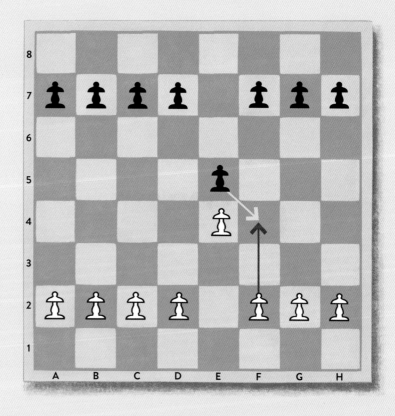

Jess: Oh yeah, because then if I take you, you take me back and you have two pawns controlling central squares.

Jamie: Exactly! Good, huh?

Jess: Well... if that's what your plan is, I'm going to put my pawn on g5 and stop you!

Jamie: Grrr! That's why I shouldn't tell you my plans!

Jess: So that is what I am going to do whenever we play now; not just think about my plans, but work out what you are going to do and stop them.

Jamie: Well, yes. That's a good idea in general, not just in Pawn Wars!

Jess: What about **sacrifices** though, Jamie? I make quite a lot of those in this game.

Jamie: What were they again?

Jess: When you give up a piece in order to get something better back. So, in Pawn Wars, I would often sacrifice a pawn in order to sneak one of mine past to get to the end.

Here I would push my pawn to g6, as no matter which black pawn took it, it would create a path for one of mine to go through.

If the h-pawn took it, I could play h6 and that would have a clear path to the end. If the f-pawn took it, then my e-pawn would have a clear path to the end. If neither pawn takes it, I can keep pushing the g-pawn!

Jamie: Oh, that's so sneaky! I will definitely be watching out now in case you offer me any 'free gifts'.

Jess: It might be too late by the time you realize, so you're going to have to try and get one step ahead of me.

Jamie: Oooh this is going to be exciting now!

REVISION TIME:

Rooks, Bishops and Queens

Jess: Those games were intense! My head feels like it's going to explode!

Jamie: Yeah, I think we overdid it a little bit. Let's do something a bit more relaxing.

Jess: We should revise the **line pieces**.

Jamie: The line pieces?

Jess: Yeah, the ones that move in straight lines – the bishops, rooks and queen.

Jamie: Oooh, the line pieces. I suppose that does make sense!

Jess: They are nice and easy to remember. The bishop only moves diagonally, the rook goes forwards, backwards and sideways, then the queen does all of those things!

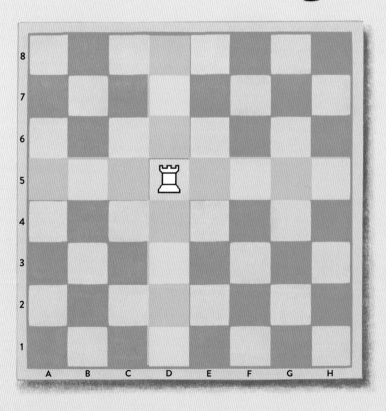

Jamie: Yeah, they are nice and simple. It is no wonder we have two of each of them!

Jess: We only have one queen!

Jamie: Unless we get a pawn to the end of the board.

Jess: Good point, smarty pants!

Jamie: At least they can travel a lot faster than the pawns!

Jess: Which is why they are more fun.

Jamie: Let's get some games of Cops and Robbers going so we can practise!

Jess: Definitely.

Cops and Robbers Strategy

Jess: Whenever we play Cops and Robbers, you ALWAYS win when you're the cop, Jamie. Why is that?

Jamie: Because robbers should not be allowed to get away with stealing, so I always make sure I catch them!

Jess: OK, silly, but how are you always so good with the pieces?

Jamie: I often beat you with the pawns too!

Jess: Exactly! You've got to teach me.

Jamie: Well, I've had a lot more practice than you, so I know some cool tricks.

Jess: Please teach me for when my friend Marnie comes round! She always rubs it in when she wins and I want to take that smug look off her face.

Jamie: OK, let's start with the queen vs. eight pawns.

It is White's turn to start and since we are already attacking the d2 pawn, it would make sense for them to push it to d3 so that we don't take it straight away. This is when it is our turn to start wreaking havoc! What sort of thing do you usually do, Jess?

Jess: I just kind of move my queen along the back rank attacking the pawn on that file.

Jamie: That's okay, but the pawns can keep pushing themselves up to a square where they are defended. Remember, if we lose our queen then we lose the game.

Jess: Well, what do you do?

Jamie: My secret weapon is the **double attack**.

Jess: Of course! Is that the same thing as a **fork**?

Jamie: Yeah! I make sure that with each move, I attack more than one pawn at a time. That way, when one of them moves to safety, I can take the other!

Jess: Oh gosh, so you've only played one move and you've already captured one of my guys!

Jamie: Yup – and when I reach your 2nd rank, I will be skewering your other pawns too!

Jess: But isn't a skewer when you attack a more valuable piece and the piece behind it is less valuable?

Jamie: Yes. This is kind of like a **skewer** too, but here the pawns have the same value.

Jess: This is so cool! I'm going to try this on Marnie.

Jamie: There is one thing you have to watch out for, though. If a pawn starts to sneak quite far down the board, don't keep munching on all the free ones further back. Make sure you can stop it before it reaches the 8th rank and promotes!

Jess: I do sometimes get a little bit greedy and forget about that. Thanks for the tips, Jamie – Marnie won't know what hit her.

REVISION TIME:
Knights

Jamie: Clippety-clop and around the corner, clippety-clop and around the corner, clippety-clop and around the corner.

Jess: What *are* you muttering, Jamie?!

Jamie: It's how the knight moves, remember?

Jess: Ah yeah, your silly rhyme!

Jamie: It helped you to remember, so shhhh.

Jess: I know, I know. I also tried to remember it a different way: one forward, then one diagonal.

Jamie: Huh?! Does that work?

Jess: Yeah... look:

Jamie: I suppose it does! And you can turn the knight around and go 'forwards' in all four directions.

Jess: Yes, so I can go one sideways, then one diagonal or one backwards then one diagonal.

Jamie: It still makes an L shape.

Jess: It always will, Jamie.

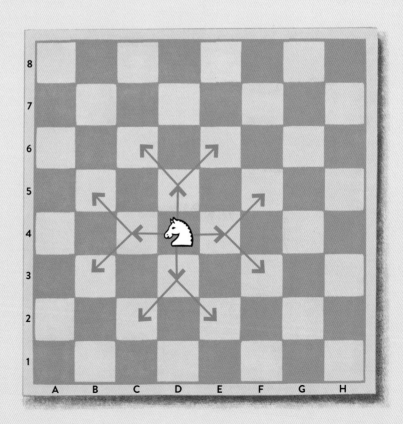

Jamie: It is still so cool how it can jump over everything in its way... like a real horse!

Jess: Yes, yes, you love horses. We get it.

Jamie: It is a bit annoying that knights can't just capture everything they jump over and that they have to land on the actual piece.

Jess: But it would be so difficult for pieces to be safe from the knight if that were the case!

Jamie: True!

Jess: Oooh, can we play Hungry Horses, please?

Jamie: Oh, but you are so good at that game, Jess!

Jess: That's why I want to play, hehe! Don't worry – it can be my turn to give you some tips!

Jamie: Fine. Let's set it up.

Hungry Horse Strategy

Jess: So the key to this game is calculation. You cannot just think of one move, but you need to plan ahead.

Jamie: I always just think of my moves as I go along.

Jess: But then you will never improve! The best chess players always calculate several moves ahead to try and stay ahead of their opponents.

Jamie: OK, so what do you suggest?

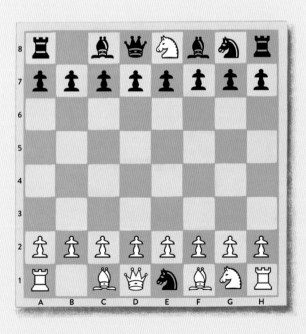

Jess: Well, this game is good practice because you don't have to calculate the opponent's moves. Remember, it is just the first person to eat all the pieces who wins. The knights are the only ones that can move and they can't be taken.

Jamie: I only ever look at my plans anyway.

Jess: That's very selfish of you, Jamie. No wonder you miss **tactics** made by your opponent.

Jamie: I know, I know. I need to learn not to be so greedy.

Jess: Not in this game... get eating!

Jamie: Yum yum! OK, so we've played two moves each and got two pieces each, but now what? I can't eat anymore, so what should I do?

Jess: You can't always take something during a game of chess, so you will often need to create an **attack** on an enemy piece to try and take it on the next go. This is the same here.

Jamie: OK, so if I play my knight back to c7, I can start to move towards the other pieces right?

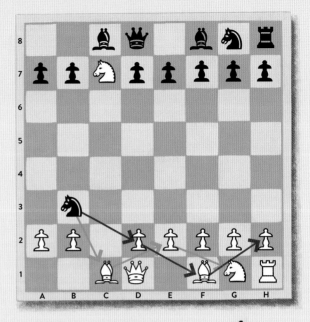

Jess: Yes, that's fine, but surely you want to try and eat something on as many goes as possible? I think I would play my knight to b3 instead. Then, I have two munching routes ahead of me!

Jamie: Smart! You really are one step ahead of me!

Jess: Ha! One? Don't insult me!

Jamie: OK show off, I will get the hang of this. I must plan ahead how to eat as many pieces in a row as possible. Give me a few games to practise and I will be Hungry Horse champion in no time!

A Knight's Tour

Jamie: OK, Miss Hungry Horse Queen... if you are so good with the knight, I have a seriously hard challenge for you.

Jess: What is it?

Jamie: It is called the Knight's Tour.

Jess: That sounds exciting... what is it?

Jamie: All you have to do is visit every square on the board with your knight in the least number of moves possible!

Jess: That sounds long!

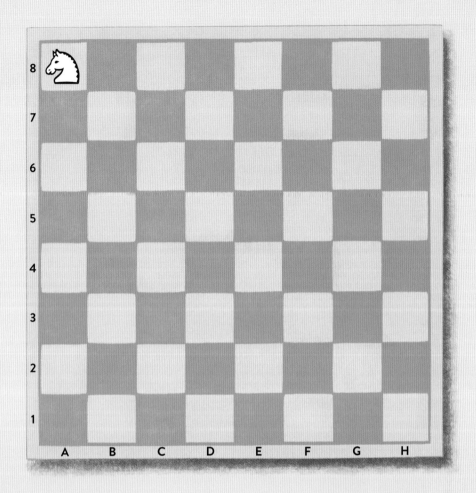

Jamie: It does take some time. It is possible to reach every square with only one visit to each square. That is the challenge!

Jess: Have you completed it?

Jamie: No, the least number of moves I have done it in is 68.

Jess: That's still pretty amazing!

Jamie: Yeah, I'm happy with it, but I just need more practice. My friend Harry has done it in 63!

Jess: How is that possible? There are 64 squares on the board, so surely 64 would be the least possible amount of moves!

Jamie: Remember, you start on a square, so you only need to visit 63 others.

Jess: Ahhh, clever! Harry is so smart!

Jamie: I know! I'm going to try to practise some more to see if I can challenge him.

Jess: Me too!

Chess Variants

How did you get on with the Knight's Tour, Jess?

Jess: Not great... I can't seem to do it in less than 72 moves.

Jamie: Keep trying. You will get better at it in no time.

Jess: I like these little games though. Chess is super fun because there are endless possibilities.

Jamie: I know! While the real game of chess is exciting and challenging, I like all the cool **variants** of chess too.

Jess: Variants?

Jamie: Yeah... like different versions of chess with different rules.

Jess: More rules? It took me long enough to remember all the original rules!

Jamie: Well, the variants are supposed to be more fun and are often a lot easier. Some are more complicated, though!

Jess: Oh gosh. I don't think I can take those that are more complicated!

Jamie: You will be fine, Jess. You will pick up the rules in no time.

Jess: I hope so.

Jamie: Let's go and find Harry and Marnie, as they know loads of really cool variants that we can all play together.

OK, sounds fun!

Jesön Mor

Marnie: Hey, Jess! How are you?

Jess: Hey, Marnie. I'm good, thanks! How is the chess study going?

Marnie: Not bad, but it is hard work. I miss my training buddy!

Jess: I know. I have been so busy. Jamie and I have been working a lot together too.

Marnie: What have you been working on?

Jess: This week, we have been working hard at mastering the knight and playing games like Hungry Horse and the Knight's Tour.

Marnie: Oh, that tour is so hard! I have only made it to 66 moves and I've tried so many times.

Jess: Oh wow – that's even better than Jamie! What did you do to get so good at it?

Marnie: I just tried it over and over again! Plus, knights are my favourite piece anyway. Cousin Tommy and I started playing this game recently with just knights because we became obsessed with them. It's called Jesön Mor.

Jess: Jesön Mor? That sounds a bit weird.

Marnie: It's actually Mongolian - it means 'nine horses'.

Jess: How do you play?

Marnie: Well, as the name suggests, we might have to collect a few extra knights because we need nine each!

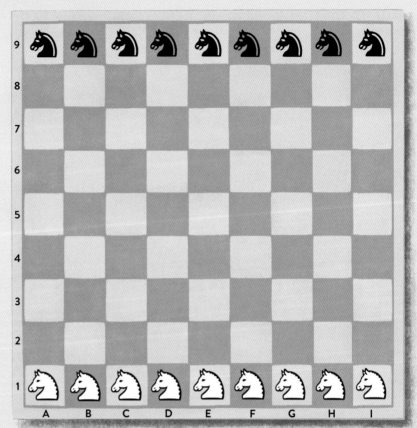

Jess: Oh gosh... let's go and raid Jamie's pieces.

Marnie: The board is set up like this:

Jess: Hang on a moment... that's a **9x9 chessboard**! Where did you get that?

Marnie: It was given to me as a present, but don't worry, we can use a normal 8x8 board and just put a knight in each corner. It won't really affect the game.

Jess: So, how does it work then?

Marnie: The aim of the game is to get a knight to occupy the e5-square and then leave the square.

Jess: That sounds super easy! Surely that's not all you have to do?

Marnie: It is a lot harder than it looks. Remember, both of you are trying to do the exact same thing, so you will be preventing each other from achieving your goal.

Jess: Of course, it is not enough to just occupy the e5-square, but you must leave it too.

Marnie: Exactly. A knight on the e5-square can be captured too or be completely blocked from moving out.

Jess: This sounds cool! I have a question, though; what if I capture all of your knights. Surely I would win then?

Marnie: Yes! That is another way to win too!

Jess: Great – let's play!!

Revision Time:
The King

Jamie: Hey, Jess. Did you and Marnie have fun yesterday?

Jess: Yeah, it was good catching up with her, but she's still much better than me at chess!

Jamie: I don't think she is; she is just very confident and sometimes that intimidates you.

Jess: Chess is a funny game like that! People can trick you into thinking they are good.

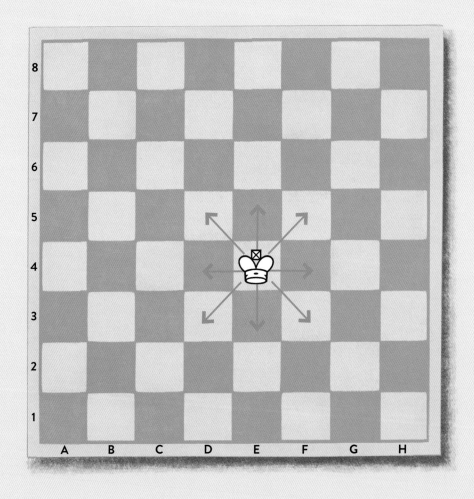

Jamie: Well, we should get back to work. We still have revision to do.

Jess: Ah yes, the king. That piece is soooo boring.

Jamie: Why? He's the most important piece on the board.

Jess: But he's so old and he can hardly move! That's so zzzz.

Jamie: That's what you may think... but the whole point of the game is to trap the king, so all the creativity around the game is based on the king.

Jess: I never really thought about it like that. OK, so enlighten me. Apart from being able to move just one square in any direction, what else do I need to bother with?

Jamie: What about the most important issue of keeping him safe? Remember the king is NEVER allowed to step into danger at any time.

Jess: Oh yeah! What was that game we played last time to practise keeping the king safe?

Jamie: Mine Alert!

Jess: Yes, let's play that again!

Mine Alert

Puzzle 1

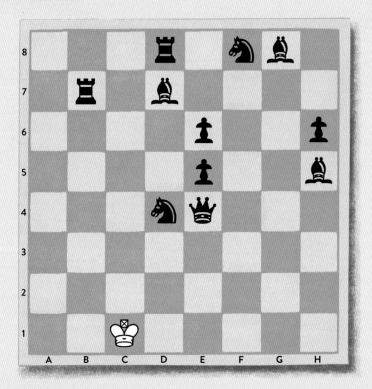

Jamie: OK, Jess, we need to always make sure our king is not in danger as it is our most important piece.

Jess: Yes, I know... this is why we **castle**, right?

Jamie: Exactly. You remember how this works, right?

Jess: Of course, we move the king two spaces towards the rook and jump the rook straight over.

Jamie: And you must not have any pieces in between the king and the rook.

Jess: I remember! Now let's get started with some exercises.

Puzzle 3

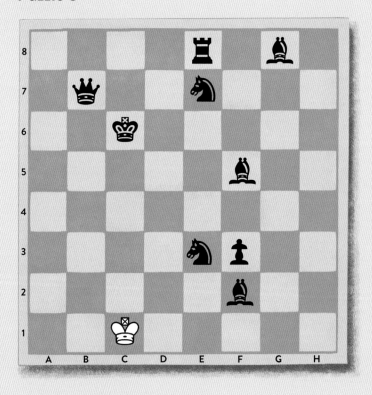

Puzzle 2

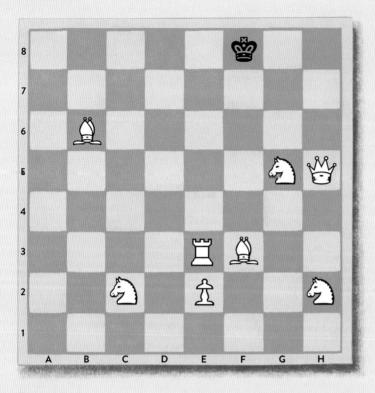

Puzzle 4

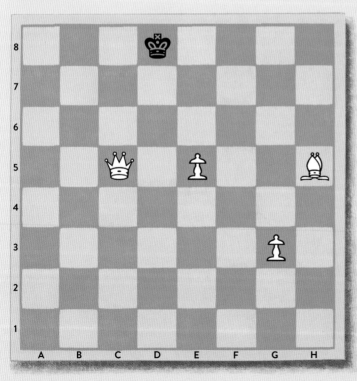

Jamie: Are we going to plan Mine Alert?

Jess: Of course, what better way to practise keeping your king safe? Remember, you cannot step on a mine (take a piece) or go to a square where another piece attacks.

Jamie: OK, I will race you to finding the correct path.

Introduction to Strategy

Jess: We've covered loads of great tips so far and it's definitely going to help me improve my game.

Jamie: Well, that's the beauty of chess. You can learn new things forever and ever. The new tricks that we have been discussing are known as **strategy**.

Jess: We talked about that in our first book.

Jamie: Yes, but only a little bit. All these ideas of planning ahead and formulating a plan of what to do are known as strategy.

Jess: I feel so sophisticated learning about strategy!

Jamie: Well, only the best chess players know about strategy.

Jess: I want to be one of the best chess players... so how exactly do I make a plan?

Jamie: A lot of things need to be thought of: what the opponent is planning on doing, what are the weaknesses in the position, which pieces are not so good.

Jess: It all sounds so complicated.

Jamie: Take a look at this position:

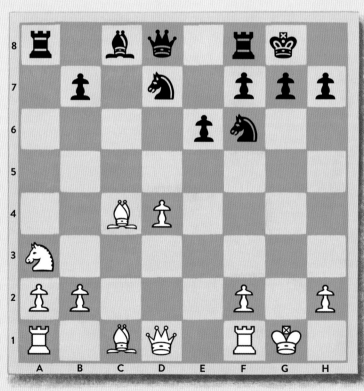

There are lots of strategical things to think about:

First of all, White has a knight on the edge of the board, where it doesn't control many squares. Then, take a look at White's king; the g-pawn is missing, which is a crucial defender, so the king may be in danger of being attacked at some point. Also, the pawn on d4 has no other pawns defending it; it is known as **isolated** and so can easily be attacked.

Black has a well-defended king so he is nice and safe, but Black's pieces are more cramped. The bishop on c8 hasn't even got any squares to move to! However, the rook on a8 has lots of squares. The fact that it has no pawn in front of it means that it is on an **open file**.

Jess: Isn't it actually a **semi-open file** because there are no black pawns but there is a white pawn on the file.

Jamie: OK, show off! The rest is correct, though.

Jess: Indeed, and this is the sort of stuff that chess grandmasters do and it helps them look so many moves ahead.

Jamie: Since they have already made a plan, it is easier to think ahead. They also know how they will respond to their opponent's move before they even play it!

Jess: So cool! I'm going to train myself to do that.

Jamie: Then we better get a move on! Too much work to do!

Strategize:
Knights vs. Bishops

Jess: Jamie, which do you prefer: knights or bishops?

Jamie: Are you kidding? You know the answer to that!

Jess: Oh yeah, how could I forget your love of horses!

Jamie: Clippety-clop and around the corner!

Jess: OK, OK! But bishops can travel must faster and further than knights.

Jamie: Faster, maybe, but not really further. They can still get to the same place, but it just takes them longer to do so.

Jess: Not in one go, they can't – knights are restricted to their clippety-clop-ness, but bishops can travel from one corner to the other in one move. Guess how many moves it takes a knight to go from one corner to the other.

Jamie: Errr... four?

Jess: Nope – six!! Such a slow old piece!

Jamie: Hey! They are awesome! Bishops can't jump and knights can jump over everything!

Jess: I suppose that is true.

Jamie: OK, here is a challenge: How many moves does it take you to capture the rook with your knight. The rook doesn't move, so take as many moves as you need.

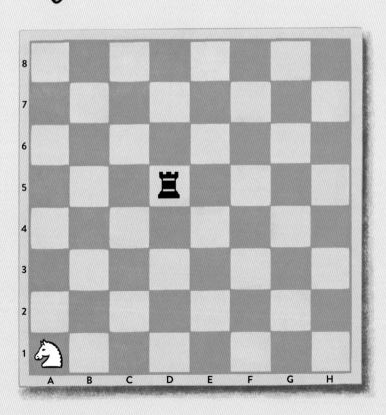

Jess: That's easy... I can do it in three moves. I can move to c2, then b4 and then take the rook.

Jamie: Or you can go to c2, then e3 and then take the rook.

Jess: Oh yeah! I forgot there are often different routes you can take. With more pieces on the board, you can pick the route that suits you.

Jamie: OK, now try this one. Do the same with your bishop. You can have as many moves as you like.

Jess: Grrrr, I've spent ages and I keep circling around it. I can't get to it.

Jamie: Haha! Do you know why?

Jess: Ohhhh gosh... it is because I have a dark-squared bishop and the rook is on a light square! I will NEVER be able to get to the rook!

Jamie: Yup, just another reason why the knight is better.

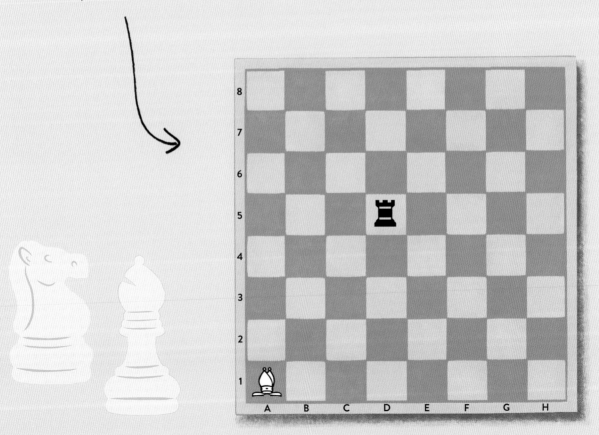

Jess: I see your point. I guess this is why knights and bishops are worth the same number of points. No one can agree which one is better!

Jamie: Maybe. Most people do prefer bishops though, because of their long-range abilities, but I just love knights because they are so complicated.

Jess: They are both great, but in different situations. Look at this position:

There is so much space on the board, the bishops have lots of room to roam free and attack pieces.

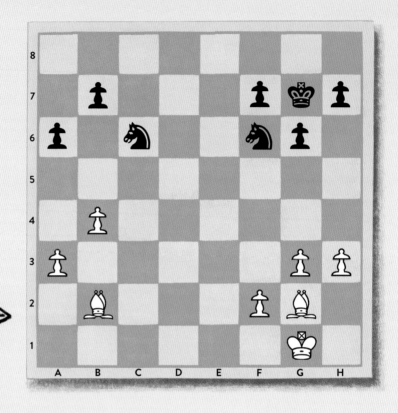

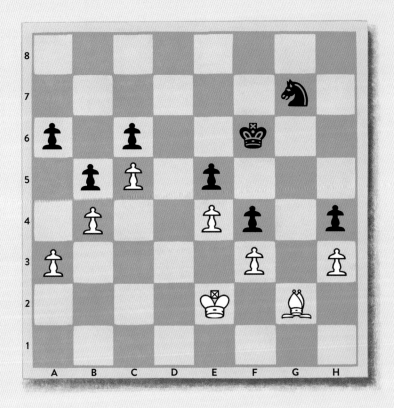

But look at this position:

It is all blocked up and there isn't much space for any of the pieces to move, so the knight's jumping power is very strong here as it can get around to places that the bishop can't reach. That's what we call great strategy.

Jamie: I do prefer knights.

Jess: OK, Jamie, but you can see situations where bishops are better, so you should appreciate them too.

Jamie: OK, I will try.

Revision Time:
Chess Notation

Jamie: Do you know what we are doing next, Jess?

Jess: What?

Jamie: **Notation** practice!

Jess: Nooooo... I hate writing down my moves!

Jamie: I know you do, but it is the sign of a good chess player when you can read and write chess notation.

Jess: But it takes so long and I always muddle up the squares.

Jamie: Again, it comes with practice. I would advise you to write down your moves every single time you even play a fun game, including against me!

Jess: Oh, I suppose it does mean that when I beat you, I have a record of it!

Jamie: Keep dreaming, Jess!

Jess: Let's remind me of all the signs and symbols again then.

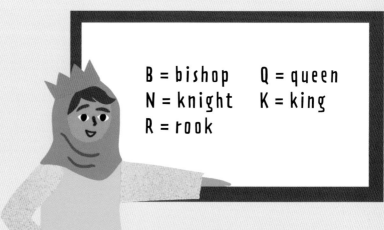

B = bishop   Q = queen
N = knight   K = king
R = rook

Jess: You missed a piece! You didn't include the P for pawn.

Jamie: That's because we don't use a letter for pawn. Instead we just write the name of the square the pawn moves to.

Jess: Oh yeah, I forgot about that! One other thing... why is the knight an N when we spell it with a K!

Jamie: Because we are already using the K for king! Since the K in knight is silent, we use N to avoid confusion.

Jess: Ahhh, that makes sense! So what about all the other notation signs? The pieces are the easy bit.

Jamie: Coming up:

Jess: Double check? What was that again?

Jamie: That was one of the tactics we looked at in the first book.

Jess: How is it possible to be checked twice at the same time? Surely that is illegal since we must move out of **check** immediately?

x	=	capture
+	=	check
0-0	=	castle kingside
0-0-0	=	castle queenside
++	=	double check
#	=	checkmate

Jamie: It is possible if it comes from a **discovered check**.

Jess: Oh yeah... it's all coming back to me now!

Jamie: Think you got the hang of this notation thing then?

Jess: I think so. I just needed a bit of revision.

Jamie: Do you remember the Classic Trick from our first book?

Jess: Of course! Scholar's Mate – it is one of the oldest tricks in the book!

Jamie: Do you think you could write it out using chess notation?

Jess: I suppose I could give it a go. It is only four moves.

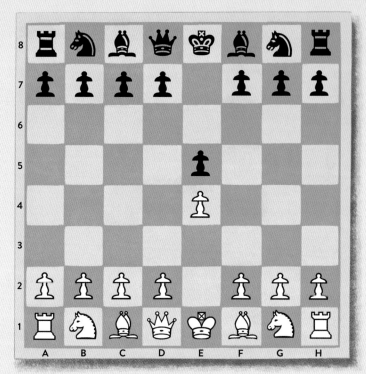

1. e4 e5

3. Bc4 Nf6

2. Qh5 Nc6

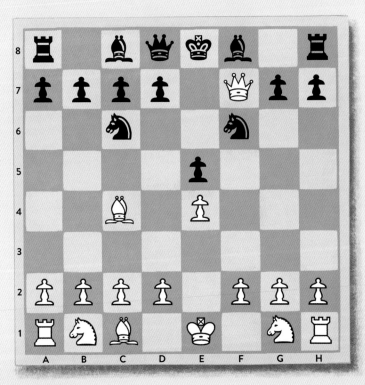

4. Qxf7#

Jamie: Nice work! You took your time though. Fancy a fun game to get you familiar with the squares?

Jess: You know I love fun games!

Co-ordinate Bingo

Jamie: Do you know what I really love doing when I am talking about chess?

Jess: What's that, Jamie?

Jamie: I love to show off by rattling off chess notation really quickly. It makes me sound super clever and really confuses a lot of people!

Jess: That doesn't sound too clever to me, Jamie. But maybe that's because I am usually one of the ones who gets confused! I can't keep up with which squares you are talking about.

Jamie: You just need practice, Jess. The more you practise your notation, the better you get.

Jess: But it doesn't seem fun to just stare at a chessboard and try to remember which square is which.

Jamie: Well, I have a really fun game which I played all the time to help me get to know the chessboard better and I guarantee that you will like it!

Jess: Oooh, I like the sound of that! Tell me more.

Jamie: Well, it is called Co-ordinate Bingo! It is just like normal bingo, but instead of having a sheet of numbers, you get a board of co-ordinates!

Jess: I LOVE BINGO!

Jamie: Well, that's good, Jess; you should be good at this game then. I will call some of our other friends and see if they want to play too. Here, you read all the rules before we start and make sure you understand everything.

Rules

e4, g7, b6!

BINGO!

1. Each player receives a unique co-ordinate bingo card with 24 different co-ordinates displayed.

2. A hat (or jar, or box, or whatever you like) of 64 pieces of paper with each co-ordinate inside is prepared.

3. Each player gets ready with a writing instrument and their bingo card.

4. The game controller picks out one co-ordinate at a time and the players mark that co-ordinate off on their card if they have it.

5. Once every co-ordinate on a player's card is crossed off, they shout BINGO and they win the game.

Jess: I understand everything, Jamie – I just want to start playing. Who else is up for it?

Jamie: Harry and Marnie both want to play too, so it should be fun watching you guys compete.

Jess: Well, I thought of some cool variations we could do on the game too, for extra fun.

Jamie: Oh yeah? Like what?

Jess: Well, before you read out exactly what co-ordinate is picked out of the hat, you could give a little clue about what the co-ordinate is and let the players guess for points. Then a little side game could be played alongside.

Jamie: Give me an example of what you mean, Jess.

Jess: Well, if you pull the co-ordinate 'f7' out of the hat, you could say: 'This is the weakest square at the beginning of the game'. Whoever answers first gets a bonus 5 points!

Jamie: Oh, that's a cool idea! OK, you, Harry and Marnie are going to play now with the bonus game alongside. Pick your co-ordinate bingo cards!

Jess: If I get a little confused, then can I write the letters and numbers on the side of the board?

Jamie: That's the whole point of the game, Jess! But OK, if you are really struggling, you can do that. After all, it is meant to be fun.

Jess: I might try designing my own bingo cards next time for good luck!

Jamie: Me too! And I might design some with fewer highlighted squares so we can get our games over and done with much quicker!

Jess: Nice plan! I bet I will win next time I play... I really got better that time and I think I won't need to write the letters and numbers on the side next time.

Jamie: OK, you're on!

Example Bingo Cards:

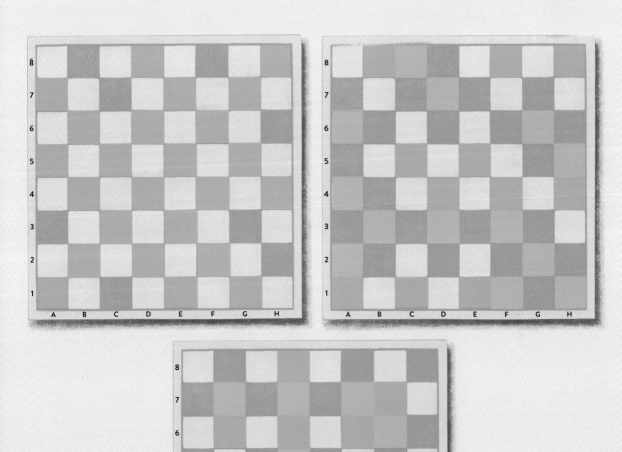

Check and Checkmate

Jess: Do you know what I miss doing?

Jamie: What's that?

Jess: Trying to kill the king.

Jamie: Haven't we been through this, Jess? You can't actually kill the king!

Jess: I know that, but I mean checkmating the king.

Jamie: But it's so difficult!

Jess: But it's the most fun thing to do. It is how you win a game after all.

Jamie: I usually try to take all of my opponent's pieces first before trying to checkmate.

Jess: That's even harder! Also, don't you also run the risk of **stalemate**?

Jamie: What was that again?

Jess: Where the king is safe on the square he stands on, but can't move anywhere and there are no other legal moves on the board.

Like this:

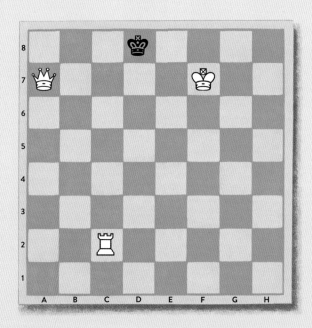

If it is Black to play, it is stalemate.

Jamie: But if it is White to play, it will be **checkmate** next move!

Jess: That's true, but it is Black to play in this position.

Jamie: Sometimes I get confused and just say it's checkmate and my opponent believes me, so shakes my hand and agrees they've lost.

Jess: That's cheating, Jamie!

Jamie: But they think it is checkmate too.

Jess: Doesn't matter. From now on, you must promise not to do that!

Jamie: Alright.

Jess: Let's revise attacking the king, so you can actually finish off your opponent instead of stalemating.

Jamie: For me, checking the king is easy. However, they can always get out of it, so checkmating feels impossible.

Jess: Well, first of all, do you remember the three ways to get out of check?

Jamie: Of course I remember my **ABC**s!

A = AVOID

I can run AWAY or AVOID the check by moving my king.

B = BLOCK

I can put a piece in between the attacker and my king.

C = CAPTURE

I can capture the piece that is checking me.

Jess: Well done! Now all you have to do is make sure your opponent can do none of these things and then it will be checkmate!

Jamie: That's a lot easier said than done!

Jess: I know that, but as you always tell me, all I need to do is practise.

Jamie: I do always say that, don't I?

Jess: Fancy taking on my checkmate challenge then?

Jamie: What is that?

Jess: Come on, I will show you!

Checkmate Challenge

Jess: The rules are really simple – you have to checkmate me in the least number of moves you can. You get all of your pieces and I only get my king!

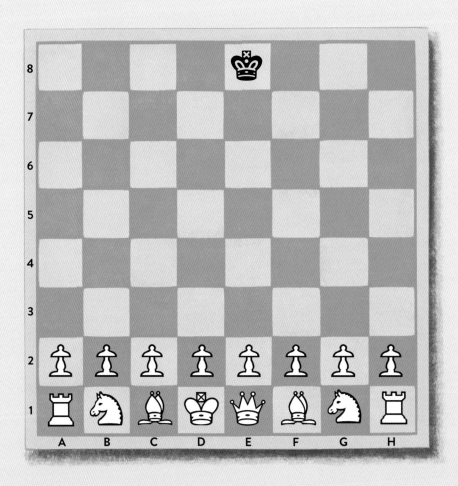

Jamie: That sounds easy enough!

Jess: Of course it is easy – I cannot win with just the king! The idea is that you use all of your pieces and not just one to attack the king. You can practise which pieces work well together and what is the best way to surround the king.

Jamie: I know that I should be forcing him to the edge of the board. That way he has fewer squares to go to and it is easier to checkmate.

Jess: Exactly. Which is why, as a defender, I am going to try and make it as hard as possible for you by staying as close to the centre as I can.

Jamie: Meanie!

Jess: You're going to do the same when it's your turn to defend!

Jamie: I suppose that is true.

Puzzle Time:

Mate in One

Jess: Wooooop! I love puzzles!

Jamie: Me too! I am buzzing after all those checkmate challenges we did.

Jess: Let's see how much better you are at checkmating and do some puzzles.

Jamie: OK. Let's do some checkmate-in-one-move puzzles. I don't think I am ready for the really complicated ones.

Jess: No problem. But let's make them harder than the ones we did in our first book. They were too easy!

Jamie: Of course – we need to challenge ourselves to get better.

Puzzle 1: White to play

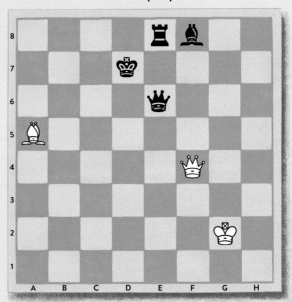

Puzzle 4: White to play

Puzzle 2: White to play

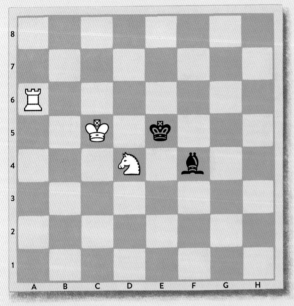

Puzzle 3: White to play

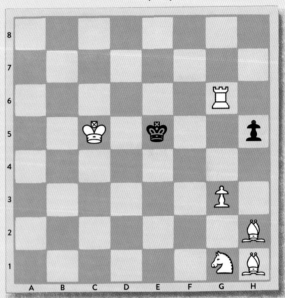

Puzzle 5: White to play

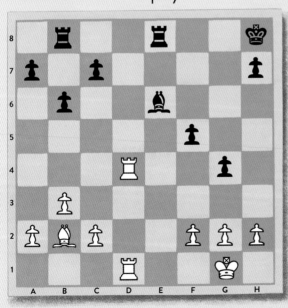

Puzzle 6: White to play

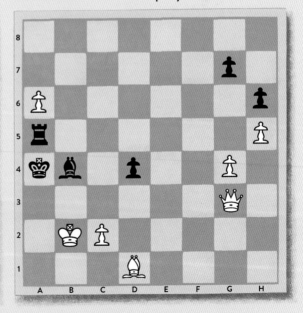

Three Check Chess

Harry: Hey, Jamie!

Jamie: Hey, Harry! It's so good to see you!

Harry: Likewise! How is your book going with Jess?

Jamie: Great, but lots of hard work. We are currently working on checkmating the king and it has got me thinking about how we always need to think about how to keep our own king safe.

Harry: That's right – it is the most important piece on the board.

Jamie: I still need to do a lot of work on it.

Harry: I know a game that we can play that should help.

Jamie: What is it?

Harry: It is called Three Check Chess and the rules are kind of self-explanatory from the name!

Jamie: Let me guess, the first person to check the opponent's king three times wins?

Harry: Exactly! Pretty simple.

Jamie: I love that idea. I was telling Jess how difficult I find it to checkmate the king, so this will be a simpler version.

Harry: That is true, but it means it is also easier for you to lose! Got to watch out for your king's safety!

Jamie: Oh no! I suppose I have to think twice about blocking in this game too, because you can just take it for another check.

Harry: Yup! Sacrificing is a big factor in this game. There will be plenty of chances to sacrifice a piece to bring the king out into the open. Since we only need to check the king three times, it may be worth it. So we will probably have some big decisions to make during the game.

Jamie: Argh, I'm so bad at making decisions!

Harry: Well, you better learn fast, because I'm really good at this game!

Jamie: Right, I need to learn to stay ahead of you and try to work out how you will attack my king and block it before you even get there.

Harry: OK, well let's see if you can do it!

Thinking Ahead

Jess: Did you have a good time with Harry?

Jamie: So much fun! Although he kept on beating me at Three Check Chess!

Jess: Marnie showed me that game – it's so much fun!

Jamie: It made me really have to think about what his plans were all the time. Something I'm not usually very good at.

Jess: That is definitely a game where you need to be aware of what your opponent is threatening. Thinking ahead is so important in chess, Jamie.

Jamie: I realize that now. The more training I do with it, the further I can think ahead.

Jess: It's an amazing skill to have.

Jamie: Sometimes I find it very tempting to just move the pieces around a bit though, because I get confused with them all moving around in my head.

Jess: Try not to, because it is all part of the training. Seeing the moves in your head is called **visualization** and it is a very powerful skill.

Jamie: What if I start to imagine pieces that aren't there? Isn't that worse? Surely, moving the pieces about is better?

Jess: Remember that when we enter tournaments, we must abide by the **touch move** rule?

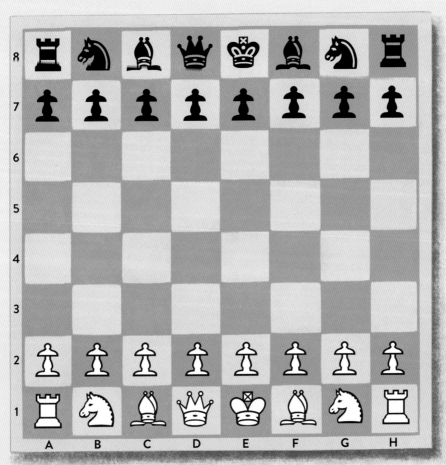

Jamie: Oh yeah... if I touch a piece, I must move it! I definitely shouldn't be moving the pieces around then!

Jess: Exactly – we need to be sure about our plan and what position it will lead to before touching anything.

Jamie: I'm going to try visualizing as far as I can now, just looking at the starting position to find out how clearly I can see.

Jess: Why not try some more checkmate puzzles, but this time, we have to see more than one move ahead?

Jamie: Good idea!

Mate in Two

Puzzle 1: White to play

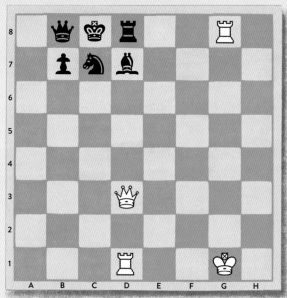

Jess: This time, we need to really visualize the positions correctly. Mate in two means that the checkmate is **forced**. So, no matter what our opponent plays, they cannot stop the checkmate.

Jamie: That sounds super hard!

Jess: It is quite hard, but remember our opponents won't just do what we want them to do, so we need to be brutal!

Jamie: Yes, no prisoners!

Jess: Thinking ahead is key here – we must look at our move, then their defence and then our checkmating move. All three must be correct and visualized before we move any pieces.

Jamie: Right, I am ready for the challenge.

Puzzle 4: White to play

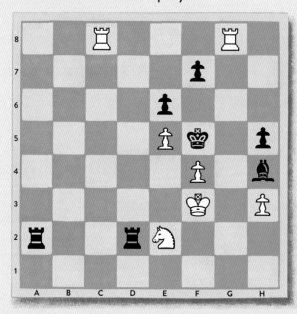

Puzzle 2: White to play

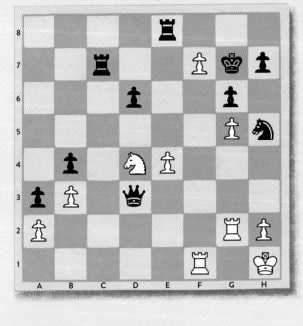

Puzzle 3: White to play

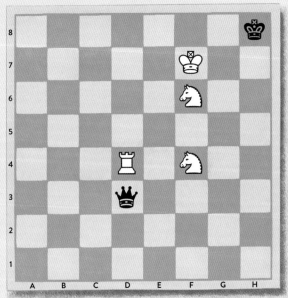

Puzzle 5: White to play

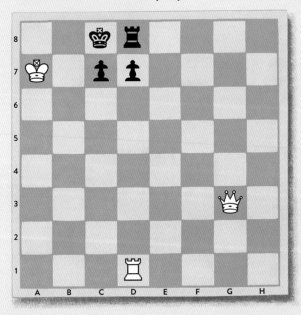

Puzzle 6: White to play

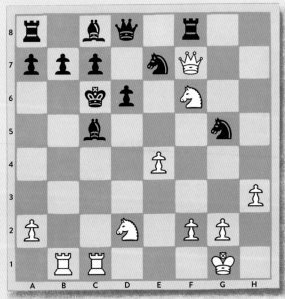

Progressive Chess

Marnie: Hey, guys!

Jamie: Hey, Marnie, how's it going?

Marnie: Great! Harry and I wanted to come visit and play some chess with you two.

Jess: We have been doing some serious visualization training, so you may not be a match for us anymore!

Harry: Oh really, Jess? I feel a challenge coming on!

Marnie: Well, I know a great game for visualization practice.

Jamie: I'm intrigued, Marnie. What is it?

Marnie: It is called Progressive Chess.

Jess: I know this! You tried to teach me before, but I gave up.

Jamie: But you have been training now so you will be better.

Harry: What are the rules?

Marnie: You take it in turns to play, with White going first as usual. However, White will start off with one move then Black will get two. White will then get three moves and Black four.

Jamie: Woah... in a row?

Harry: So I get to do all those moves without you even reacting? I can probably take all of your pieces in that time!

Marnie: Not if I take yours first! Remember, your opponent will always get one extra move than you! A lot can be done with all those moves!

Jess: I remember how difficult this was! She suddenly just checkmated me out of nowhere. She's really good...

Marnie: Thanks, Jess. It's because I take my time and calculate absolutely everything. I don't just get greedy and go for the pieces, but I actually calculate how to checkmate the king.

Jamie: Well, this definitely sounds like lots of fun. How about the four of us have a little Progressive Chess tournament between ourselves?

Harry: I'm in!

Jess: Me too!

Marnie: You're all going down!

Revision Time:
Scoring Points

Jamie: Those were the hardest games I have ever played in my life!

Jess: Me too! My head hurts!

Jamie: Please can we do something easier now? My brain needs a bit of rest.

Jess: Why don't we do some more revision? How about the value of the pieces?

Jamie: That's an easy topic.

Jess: You just asked for easy!

Jamie: That's true! It is always good to revise.

Jess: We also know why knights and bishops are worth about the same number of points now!

Jamie: I still prefer knights!

Jess: We know, Jamie. All of these points are just a rough guide anyway. Remember when we talked about strategy and we talked about how it is better to occupy central squares. Pieces are going to be stronger if they have more squares to go to too.

Jamie: That's true. The points guide is good for when you are deciding whether or not you should go in for a piece trade.

Jess: It is great for that. We should probably do some chess maths to get in form for battle.

Jamie: Nice idea – I want to be super quick at calculating points so I am going to do lots of puzzles.

Chess Maths

Jamie: So, I'm going to give you a set of easy chess maths problems to start off with so that you warm up.

Jess: OK, I like the sound of easy.

Jamie: Right, here we go:

1. $\text{♜} + \text{♞} + \text{♝} + \text{♟} \text{♟} \text{♟} = ?$

2. $(\text{♛} + \text{♞} \text{♞}) \div \text{♝} = ?$

3. $(\text{♜} \text{♜} + \text{♝} + \text{♟}) \div (\text{♟} \text{♟}) = ?$

4. $(\text{♛} + \text{♟}) \times (\text{♜} + \text{♟} \text{♟} \text{♟}) = ?$

5. $(\text{♝} \times \text{♞}) + \text{♛} = ?$

1. Rook + Knight + Bishop + 3 pawns = ?

2. (Queen + 2 Knights) ÷ Bishop = ?

3. (2 Rooks + Bishop + pawn) ÷ (2 pawns) = ?

4. (Queen + pawn) x (Rook + 3 pawns) = ?

5. (Bishop x Knight) + King = ?

Good Capture / Bad Capture?

Jess: All that maths was great to get us into shape for calculating points, but I now want to do some puzzles from actual chess positions to see if I can work out which pieces are good to take and which are bad.

Jamie: OK, I will set up a couple. In each position, there will be lots and lots of captures for both sides. You have to write down each capture and tell me if it is good or bad.

Jess: What if it is just a swap? For example, a bishop for a bishop?

Jamie: Then, you can just write 'exchange'.

Jess: OK, sounds easy enough.

Jamie: Remember to look at what they would do in return, so you can see if you gain or lose points from the trade. In fact, to give you extra work, you need to write down how many points you would gain or lose from each piece trade too!

Jess: Oh great, thanks for the extra work!

Jamie: No problem. Now get to work!

Puzzle 1

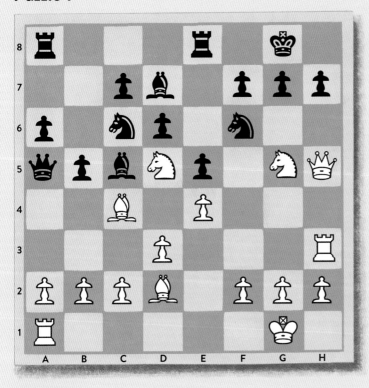

Puzzle 2

Jess: OK, well that took a while, but I am definitely going to be on the alert for captures whenever I play now.

Jamie: That was the idea.

Giveaway Chess

Jamie: You really worked me hard there, Jess!

Jess: I know, but it is all worth it!

Jamie: I feel very confident about looking for captures now!

Jess: Glad to hear it because your prize for working so hard is another fun variant game.

Jamie: Oh goodie!

Jess: You need to really be on the ball with the captures in this game. It is called Giveaway Chess.

Jamie: So, you just give away all your pieces??

Jess: Exactly! The first person to give away all their pieces wins!

Jamie: How exactly is that going to work?

Jess: We take it in turn to move the pieces as normal, but we should be looking out for how to put our pieces where they can be captured. If one of our pieces can be captured, we say, 'Take Me!' and then our opponent *must* take them.

Jamie: What if we don't want to take them?

Jess: You have to! Those are the rules!

Jamie: OK, so after I take you, is it then my turn to try and give something away?

Jess: Nope! Your capture counts as your turn, just as it would in a normal game of chess.

Jamie: That's not fair! Then you will keep saying, 'Take Me' forever!

Jess: Not necessarily. If I can capture you at any point, you can also say, 'Take Me' back.

Jamie: Nice! I have a question. What if you say, 'Take Me' after moving a piece, but I can take another piece. Can I take that one instead, or do I have to take the one you moved?

Jess: Very good question! You can actually take any piece that can be taken. That is where the game gets complicated. You must choose the piece that will suit your needs better. I would always take the piece that allows them to attack more of my pieces! Take a look at this position:

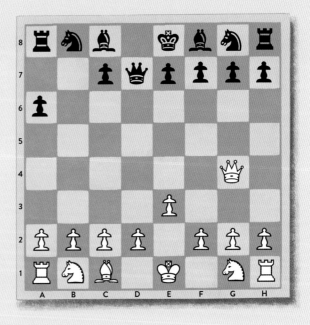

It is Black's move. White has just moved the queen to g4, hoping that Black will take it. If they do that, the black queen will probably have to take a bunch of other white pieces. However, Black can choose to take the pawn on d2 instead. Then the white queen may decide to take one of the other black pieces and it could turn into a very crazy game.

Jamie: Another question – what about the kings? We can't take kings in chess!

Jess: Another good question, Jamie! Well, there are two ways of playing this variant. We can either treat checks normally (as in, we must move out of check when we can) and then leave the kings to be captured last, or, we can just treat the king as any normal piece and throw it in to be taken whenever we want!

Jamie: I prefer to just treat the king as a normal piece.

Jess: Me too, it is easier and more fun that way.

Jamie: OK, let's play!

Opening Principles

Jess: Do you remember when you said that the beginning of the game is like a race for all the pieces to get out?

Jamie: Of course – first impressions are key. I make sure that I put my pieces on good squares at the beginning of the game so that my opponent starts to get scared!

Jess: Well, I want to scare Marnie when I play her. She is so good and she seems to be fearless at the board. If I start off with some really impressive moves, she might begin to get worried and make some mistakes in the **middlegame**.

Jamie: Why don't we take the things we learned in the first book and develop them a little bit further then?

Jess: I would like that. I know that if we control the centre, we control the game.

Jamie: That is definitely one of the most important rules. All of your pieces should aim towards the centre. However, your opponent is going to try and do the same thing as you, so they are not going to make life easy for you.

Take a look at this position:

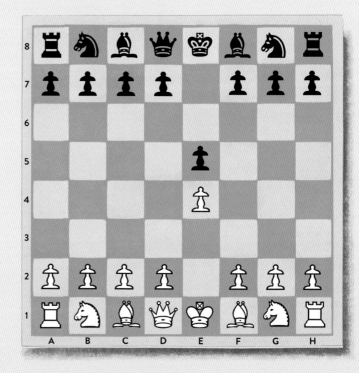

White has played their pawn to e4 as it lets the bishop out and gets control of the centre. However, Black has done the same thing and pushed their pawn to e5! That is because it is equally as good as White's move! Now, perhaps you may not want to put another pawn in the centre in case it is taken.

Jess: Remember we said that we should be getting our pieces out as quickly as possible? Especially our **minor pieces**.

Jamie: Remind me what minor pieces are again?

Jess: The minor pieces are the knights and bishops. I always get out my knights before my bishops, though.

Jamie: Why?

Jess: Because I know where my knights want to go. They want to go towards the centre. The bishops have a few good squares to choose from, so I wait until my opponent has made some moves first and then I decide where to put my bishops.

Jamie: I see your point. So you have played your knight to f3... I will put my knight to h6.

Jess: That's not a very good move, Jamie!

Jamie: Why not?

Jess: Because knights on the rim are dim!

Jamie: Huh?

Jess: A knight on the side has no pride.

Jamie: You're a poet and you don't know it!

Jess: But I do know it! These are little rhymes to help me remember that my knights belong in the centre of the board. Remember... the octopus knight?!

Jamie: Oh gosh, yes! A knight in the centre controls eight squares, but on the side of the board it only controls four.

Jess: When it gets into the corner, it only controls two!

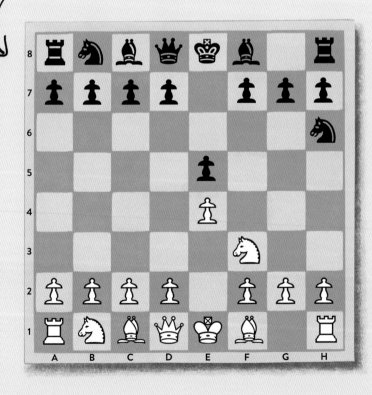

Jamie: You better warn her before going in the corner!

Jess: That rhyme doesn't work, Jamie.

Jamie: Yes it does!

Jess: Why is the knight female?

Jamie: It just is, OK!

Jess: Well, fine. Just take back your move and play something better. You should also notice that my knight on f3 is attacking your pawn on e5. You might want to defend that!

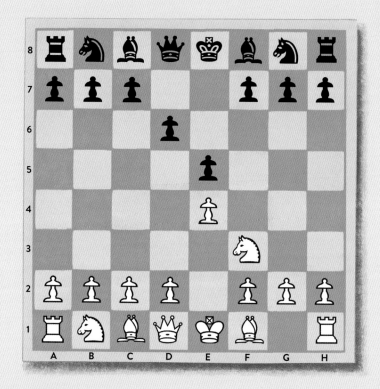

Jamie: OK, then I will put my pawn to d6.

Jess: This is OK, but now you are blocking in your poor bishop on f8. He is not happy about that!

Jamie: So what would you suggest, Jess?

Jess: I would put my knight to c6 as not only is that putting a knight towards the centre, it is also defending the pawn on e5.

Jamie: I like that move!

Jess: OK, castling is my next plan, so I am going to move my bishop out so I have room to castle.

Jamie: OK, I am going to bring my queen out.

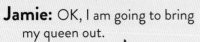

Jess: Thanks for the free queen!

Jamie: What?! Nooooo!

Jess: Well, that teaches you for bringing out your best soldier so early! Even if she doesn't get taken, your queen is so valuable and all the other little soldiers will be trying to hunt her down so she does get trapped. If she somehow escapes, she will still have lost so much time running around trying to find shelter.

Jamie: You're right – that was very silly of me. I will stick to developing my pieces and castling.

Jess: Remember when you used to try and make pretty patterns with your pawns as your **opening** choice?

Jamie: Yes! I thought it was really cool, but in fact I just made loads of holes so the enemy could get in.

Jess: Yeah and you left all your best soldiers at home in bed and only fought with your weak ones.

Jamie: I've come a long way since then though, Jess.

Jess: Yes you have, Jamie. Fancy doing some puzzles to test how much you know about your opening principles now?

Jamie: Why not?

Puzzle Time:

Yes, No or Maybe

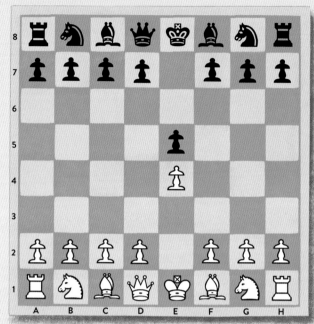

A) Nf3 **B)** Na3 **C)** Bb5

Jess: OK, the aim of the puzzles is to pick the best moves to play in the opening stages of the game. In each position, there will be three moves to choose from and you just have to say yes, no or maybe to each one.

Jamie: Do I have to pick one of each?

Jess: No, you can say yes to each one if you like. Just remember that you want to pick moves that help you develop your pieces and get you castled, etc.

Jamie: No problem. Bring on the puzzles.

Puzzle 3: White to play

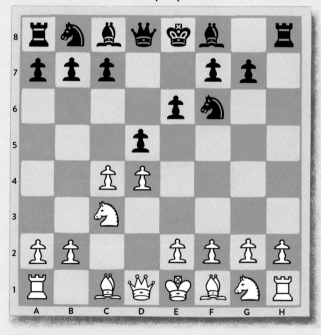

A) Bg5 **B)** h3 **C)** c5

Puzzle 2: White to play

A) Nc3   **B)** Bc4   **C)** Bb5+

Puzzle 4: Black to play

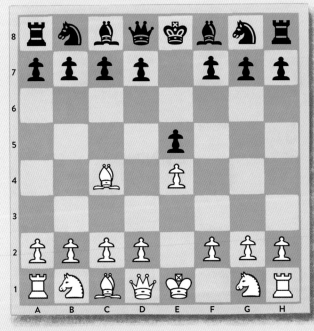

A) Qh4   **B)** Nh6   **C)** d5

Yes!

Maybe!

No!

Revision Time:
Pins, Forks and Skewers

Jamie: Right, Jess, time for some difficult stuff: TACTICS! I love tactics!

Jess: Me too! I bet I know which one is your favourite.

Jamie: Forks! Definitely forks!

Jess: That's because knights are amazing at forks.

Jamie: Indeed they are! Nothing can move like a knight, so they can easily attack pieces without them attacking them back.

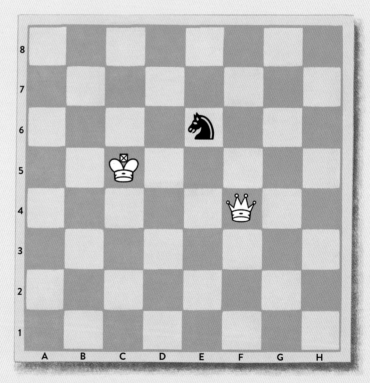

Royal Fork

Jess: Forks are pretty cool. You attack more than one piece at the same time with your piece. Therefore, even if they move one to safety, you can take the other.

Jamie: What about **pins** and **skewers** though? They're still pretty cool.

Jess: Yeah, that's what the line pieces are good for!

Jamie: Were they the bishops, rooks and queens?

Jess: Yup – the ones that all control straight lines.

Jamie: I get confused between a pin and a skewer. Which was which again?

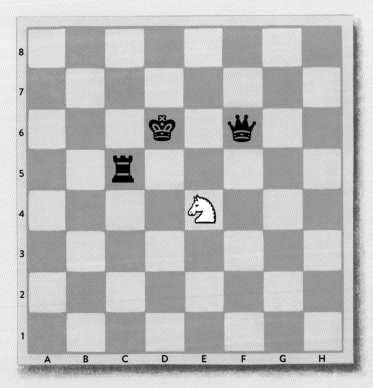

Family Fork

Jess: A pin is where you stop a piece from moving. There are two types of pin:

An **absolute pin** is where you attack a piece and the king is on the same line as the piece, so if it moves out of the way, it will be check. Therefore, the piece is *absolutely* pinned to that square.

A **relative pin** is where you attack a piece and a more valuable piece is behind it. The piece can be moved, but it probably wouldn't be wise to do so. Therefore, it is *relatively* pinned to the square it is on.

Jamie: Pins seem so annoying! Imagine not being able to move your pieces!

Jess: Exactly! That's why you should try to break the pins as soon as you can.

Absolute Pin

Relative Pin

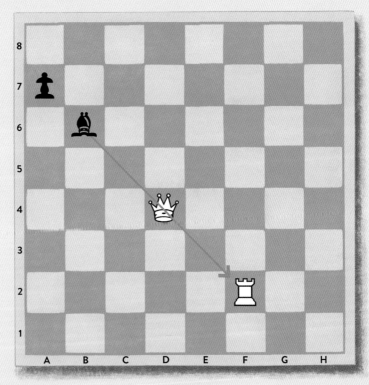

Skewer

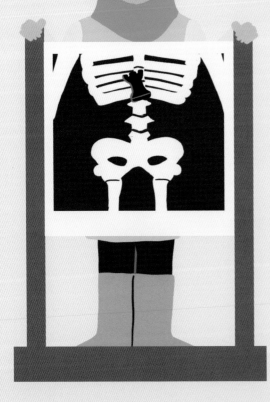

Jamie: So, what were skewers again?

Jess: A skewer is a bit like a backwards pin. The stronger piece is actually in front, so when you move that one to safety, the one behind it can be taken.

This is also known as an **x-ray** as you are looking through the first piece, only to get to the one behind it.

Jamie: When I watch grandmasters play, I see these tactics in every single one of their games. No wonder they are so good!

Jess: That's why we need to practise spotting them! Come on, Harry and Marnie want to play a tactics game with us.

SPAF

Harry: Hey, guys! Ready for some fun with tactics?

Jamie: Always! What do you have in mind?

Marnie: We play this game called SPAF.

Jess: SPAF? What on earth is that? It sounds really weird.

Marnie: It stands for Skewers, Pins And Forks!

Jess: Ohhhh, that would make sense.

Jamie: So, how do we play?

Harry: Basically, we just play a normal game of chess, but we get rewarded for any tactics that we see. The more we see, the more points we get. The person with the most points at the end is the winner.

Marnie: We run SPAF tournaments. As soon as someone does a pin, fork or skewer, they have to put up their hand. If they name the tactic correctly, they get points.

Jess: That sounds really fun!

Harry: Remember, the aim of the game is not to checkmate, but to create the tactics. So, no bonus points for checkmating early.

Jamie: Fine by me, I prefer to do tactics anyway!

Marnie: How about you and Jess play and Harry and I will be the arbiters first and award you points? Then we switch once you have the hang of it?

Jess: Sounds good. What is the scoring system?

Harry: You can use anything, but this is what we use:

Jamie: Let's play! I'm going to drag the game out as long as possible so I can get more tactics points.

Jess: Not as many as me!

POINTS

Standard fork.........................1 point

Fork to win **material**...............2 points

Royal/Family fork..................3 points

Pin......................................1 point

Correctly named as
absolute/relative.............1 bonus point

Skewer.............................2 points

Skewer to win material...........3 points

Checkmating opponent...........5 points

REVISION TIME:
More Tactics

Discovered Check

Jess: That was so much fun!

Jamie: Only because you won!

Jess: Hehe, well that did help.

Jamie: Well, I want to do some harder tactics then.

Jess: Alright. How about we look at some of those discovered attacks/checks?

Jamie: Oooh I like those – they are really sneaky!

Jess: What was the difference between the two of them, though?

Jamie: Well, a discovered check is when you move a piece, but the piece behind it is actually the one giving the check, not the piece you moved.

Then a **discovered attack** is the same thing, but the piece behind doesn't actually give a check, but just attacks a piece.

You should always move the piece to the square that does the most damage. It usually doesn't matter if it is attacked, especially in a discovered check.

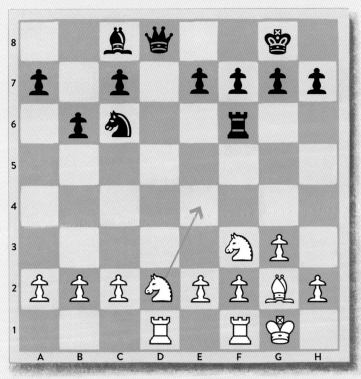

Discovered Attack

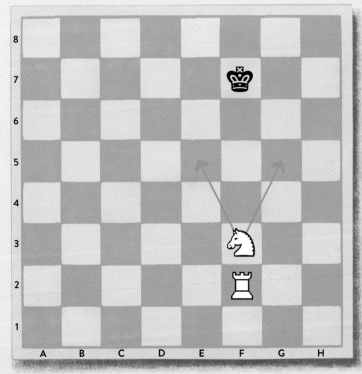

Double Check

Jess: I have a question, though. What if the piece you move also gives a check, as well as the piece behind it? Then, isn't the king in check twice?

Jamie: Yes, that is a double check. It is the only possible way to get a king in check with two pieces at the same time.

Jess: Can you give a triple check?

Jamie: Not legally, no. If you somehow find yourself being checked three times, you probably forgot to move your king out of check at some point!

Jess: I would never do that! I have practised keeping my king safe too much!

Jamie: Do you remember the **removing the defender** tactic?

Jess: Of course, it is one of the most useful tactics.

Jamie: Indeed. It always comes up in my games.

Jess: Whenever I want to do something, but my opponent is stopping me, I just look for the piece that is stopping me and I get rid of it!

Jamie: But sometimes you can't just take it off the board.

Jess: Right, but I can drive it away.

I want to take the pawn on c7 with my knight, so I can fork the king and rook, but the knight on d5 is stopping me. So, perhaps if I play my pawn to e4, the knight will move and then I can take c7!

Jamie: I like it when we sacrifice to remove a defender.

Jess: Me too! People don't see it coming because they think that we are giving them a free gift, but in fact we are setting a trap.

Jamie: Look at the one I did the other day:

I'm White and I used my rook to take the knight on f6. My opponent got so excited and snapped my rook off the board, but didn't see my real **threat**. I wanted to take the pawn on h7 with my queen delivering checkmate. The beauty of this sacrifice is that, no matter which way Black takes my rook, it will be checkmate!

Jess: Ouch! That must have hurt.

Jamie: It felt good to me!

Spot the Tactic

Jess: I need some practice with those tactics as they are quite difficult.

Jamie: Yeah, I could do with some too. I found a bunch that we could do. They are all either discovered attacks/checks or some sort of removing the defender tactics.

Jess: Let's do them together!

Puzzle 1: Black to play

Puzzle 4: White to play

Puzzle 2: Black to play

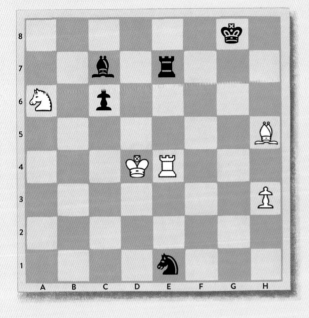

Puzzle 3: White to play

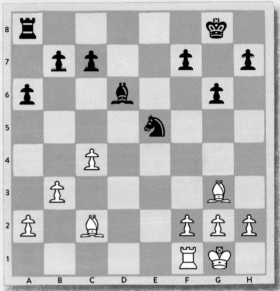

Puzzle 5: Black to play

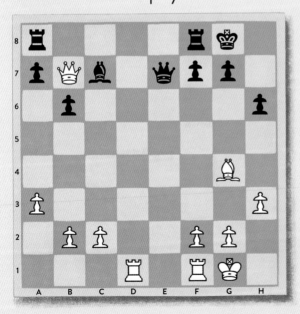

Puzzle 6: Black to play

Spot the Threat, Stop the Threat

Jamie: They were really useful. I feel a lot more confident now!

Jess: Me too! However, we knew what kind of tactics we were supposed to be looking for. In a real game, there is no one there to tell us what to look for.

Jamie: Also, it is all well and good knowing how to attack our opponents with these tactics, but what if they try it on us?

Jess: I think I need some practice at defending.

Jamie: I agree. I need to practise spotting when my opponent is threatening something and then doing something about it.

Jess: Let's try the following exercises. We need to spot what our opponent is threatening and then find the best way to defend against it.

Jamie: Remember, sometimes attack is the best form of defence!

Puzzle 1: Black to play

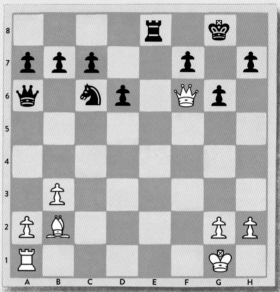

Puzzle 4: White to play

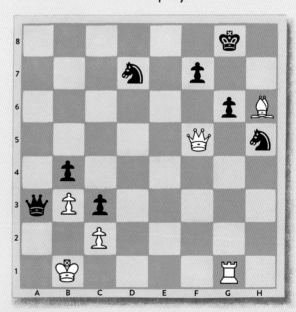

Puzzle 2: White to play

Puzzle 3: Black to play

Puzzle 5: White to play

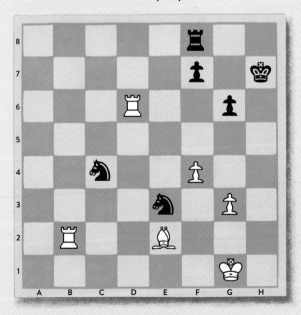

Puzzle 6: White to play

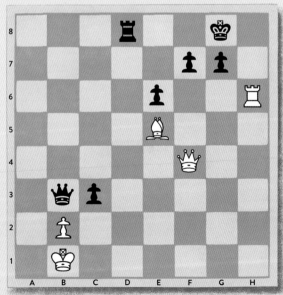

Walking the Dog Challenge

Jamie: Do you remember how I showed you my technique of Walking the Dog in the first book?

Jess: Yes, the checkmate with two rooks!

Jamie: I have been playing in some tournaments where they use the chess clocks and I have been getting to a position where I have the two rooks, but I have hardly any time left on my clock. I then panic and usually end up losing one of the rooks!

Jess: Oh no! That's not good! The two rooks checkmate is the easiest one of the lot. You should be able to do that with your eyes closed.

Jamie: But how would I see where the pieces are to move them?

Jess: It's a saying, Jamie! I don't actually mean with your eyes closed. I think you need to do some challenges to practice your endgame skills.

Jamie: What sort of challenges?

Jess: Marnie and I do timed challenges against each other. We only allow ourselves 1 minute on the clock and we have to checkmate each other as fast as possible. We actually have reduced our times to 30 seconds now because we have become so good at it.

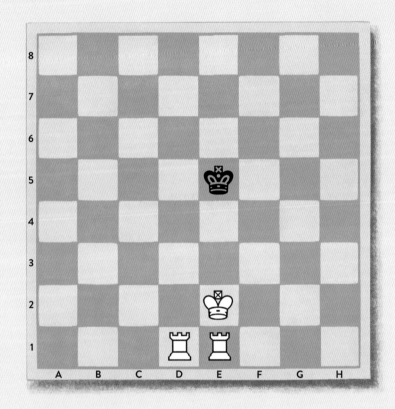

Jamie: No way! 30 seconds for the entire checkmate? What position do you start in?

Jess: We set up the two rooks one like this:

If you lose a rook, you start again! It should be really simple. It is just a good way to make sure you *really* know your checkmates.

Jamie: OK, let's try it!

Shadow Mate Challenge

Jamie: That really helped, you know, Jess!

Jess: I told you it would! Ready for a harder one?

Jamie: The queen checkmate?

Jess: Yup! This has definitely got to be the most popular one of them all. Endgames usually end up with just pawns on the board and maybe a couple of other pieces, but it is a race to get one to the end safely to promote to a queen.

Jamie: Yeah, then the queen goes round eating all the remaining pieces ready to give the **kiss of death**.

Jess: Do you think you can checkmate me in under a minute with just the queen?

Jamie: I need to remember the shadow technique; it was so good.

Jess: And you need to remember to avoid stalemate!

Jamie: Of course! I can do this. Set the board up.

Jess: Let's start from here. You have one minute. Actually, you should be good enough to do it in 30 seconds.

Jamie: Challenge accepted!

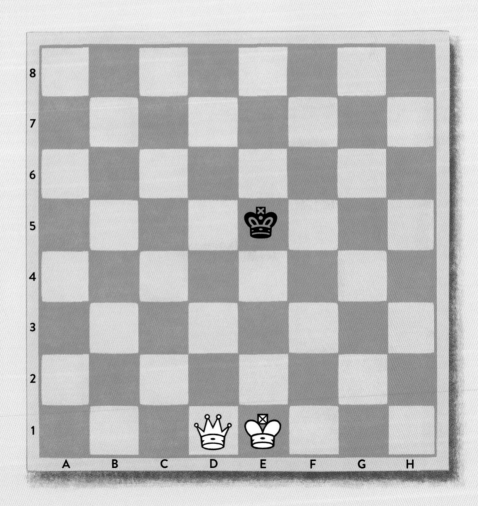

Box 'em in Challenge

Jamie: I am the king of checkmates!

Jess: Steady on! You've started with the easiest ones! Let's see how you do with just one rook.

Jamie: That one is super hard though!

Jess: Just remember the key rule: if you can make the box smaller, you should. If not, move your king.

Jamie: Move your king to where?

Jess: Well, there won't be too many options! Most of the time, you will have to stay in contact with the rook. Move it towards the opponent's king, so that you can close the box on the next move.

Jamie: I always seem to let it escape!

Jess: Just keep the box as small as possible. Beware of stalemate when the king is near the corner.

Jamie: OK, let's just do this. I'm going to need lots of practice.

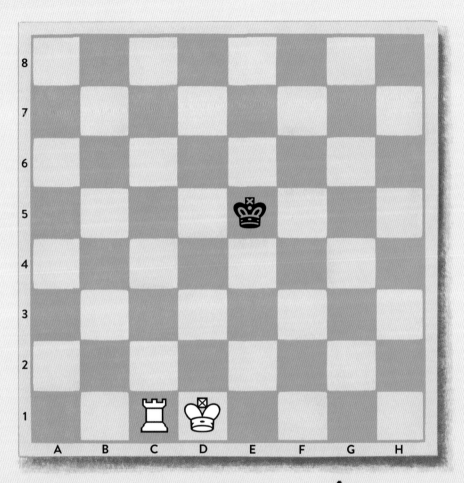

Jess: I've set the board up now. If you want,
I can go first to remind you of the technique.

Jamie: Yes, please. I will try to defend as well
as I can.

GAME TIME:
Guess the Move

Jamie: We have worked so hard, Jess, and done all this training.

Jess: I know, I feel like I have really improved.

Jamie: Are you ready to start looking at some grandmaster games?

Jess: Ohhh I don't think I am ready for that yet!

Jamie: Come on – where's your fighting spirit?

Jess: OK. Well, what do I have to do?

Jamie: We are going to play 'Guess the Move'. All you have to do is guess all of White's moves. You get points for each answer you guess correctly. We will total up your score at the end and work out just how awesome you are!

Jess: That doesn't sound too bad. But how am I supposed to think like a GM?

Jamie: I'm not expecting you to get all of the moves, but that is the challenge!

Jess: I suppose I have worked really hard to get this far. Let's give it a go.

Jamie: OK, the game is between Reti and Tartakower and it took place in Vienna in 1910. They are two of the greatest chess players to have ever lived.

∙∙∙

Richard Reti vs. Saviely Tartakower
Vienna, 1910

Jamie: I will give you the first move – 1. e4

Jess: I could have got that! Most top players usually either play 1. e4 or 1. d4 as their first move, so it was going to be one of those two moves!

Jamie: That's true, although there are other good starting moves too. Do you know why some people move their pawn in front of their queen first instead of the one in front of their king?

Jess: Is it because it is safer?

Jamie: Sort of; the pawn is already defended by the queen, so that does make it safer. Usually, games started like this lead to what we call **closed positions**.

Jess: Closed? So no one is allowed in?

Jamie: Again, sort of! There is just much less room to move in closed positions. Games started with 1. e4 usually lead to more **open positions** where the pieces have much more room to move.

Jess: OK, so it is just a matter of taste?

Jamie: Exactly – they are both good moves. It just depends what type of game you are in the mood for.

Jess: Well, what did Tartakower play in this position?

Jamie: He played 1...c6

Jess: That looks like a rubbish move!

Jamie: Why?

Jess: Because he is not controlling the centre!

Jamie: Well, actually, it is not such a bad move, because he will play the move ...d5 next and then he will have control of the centre.

Jess: But surely that is not as good as a move like 1...e5?

Jamie: Again, it is a matter of opinion. This opening is known as the **Caro-Kann Defence** and is just one of many many openings that people can choose to play. It leads to a **semi-open position**.

Jess: Why only half open?

Jamie: Because Black doesn't immediately put a pawn in the centre, the positions lead to quite open positions, but not as open as after a move like 1...e5 or 1...c5.

Jess: OK, well I am going to guess that White plays 2. d4 now.

Jamie: Why have you chosen that move?

Jess: If my opponent lets me put two pawns in the centre, I will!

Jamie: Well, I think Reti felt the same way!

Jess: Yay... how many points?

Jamie: 2 points for getting that correct and no points for guessing Black's next move!

Jess: You already told me – **2...d5**

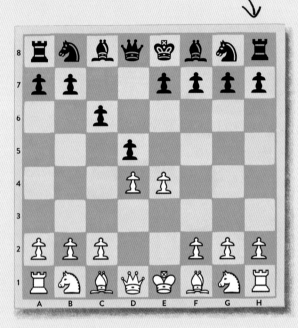

Jamie: You have lots of choices now – how will you choose to continue?

Jess: Well, my pawn on e4 is being attacked, so I have four options right?

A = Avoid
B = Block
C = Capture
D = Defend

Jamie: You also have Counterattack! Those are the five pillars of the defence. I sometimes think of them as ABCDE:

A = Avoid
B = Block
C = Counterattack
D = Defend
E = Eat

Jess: Ohhhhh – eat! How funny! OK, I will think of it like that – how clever!

Jamie: Well, what is your choice?

Jess: OK, I think I will defend with my knight. I will play **3. Nc3** because it is defending the pawn but it is also developing a piece to a good square.

Jamie: That is also what Reti played! Great start so far, Jess! Another two points!

Jess: Thanks!

Jamie: There are lots of sensible moves here, but this is what Reti played.

Jess: And what did Tartakower do?

Jamie: He took the pawn on **3...dxe4**

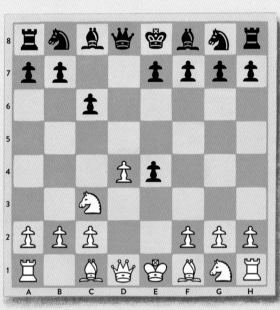

Jess: But that doesn't help him develop! Surely he should be getting a piece out instead?

Jamie: Maybe, but he also doesn't like White having two pawns in the centre, so he is trying to get rid of one. Maybe he can gain some time by developing on the next move with 4...Bf5 and at the same time attacking White's knight.

Jess: Ah, that's a nice idea. Well, my move is easy: **4. Nxe4**

Jamie: Only 1 point this time – that was too easy. Tartakower now chose to develop his knight to **4...Nf6**

Jess: I don't mind that move because it at least develops a piece and helps him get closer to castling.

Jamie: Yes, but I remember Harry teaching me something about **doubled pawns**.

Jess: What are they?

Jamie: It is when you have two pawns on the same file as each other. They are not so good because they block each other from moving. This was a positional strategy Harry taught me.

Jess: Oh and if White takes the knight on f6 now, then Black will have to get doubled pawns! Thanks, Jamie, I am going to do that!

Jamie: Just because it is a good move, doesn't mean Mr Reti played it!

Jess: Ohhhh no! Then I change my mind.

Jamie: Too late! No going back! Don't rush your moves remember... and don't play moves just because someone else suggests them! Use your own brain!

Jess: Ok, Jamie. What did he play then?

Jamie: He played 5. Qd3

Jess: What? Why? That breaks a lot of rules! You are bringing your queen out early and you are also blocking the path for the light-squared bishop to develop.

Jamie: Reti had a plan though; he wanted to castle queenside and develop a nice big attack.

Jess: Oh, I suppose it does help him castle queenside. Wait though, I see a pin for Black! 5...Bf5!

Jamie: Jess, that's a blunder!

Jess: Why? You pin and you win!

Jamie: Because every tactic comes from an undefended piece remember... and your bishop is undefended!

Jess: Uh-oh! You're right... I feel something nasty coming.

Jamie: Yes – a discovered attack!

Jess: I see it!!! If White takes the knight on f6, it is check! Then, whichever way Black takes back, White can take the undefended bishop on f5.

Jamie: Well done, Jess!

Jess: I didn't see it at first because I assumed that the knight was pinned on e4 and couldn't move.

Jamie: That is why it is known as a relative pin, because it usually doesn't want to move, but in this case, a check must be dealt with, so it is safe to move.

Jess: Very clever. I'm guessing Tartakower didn't play such a bad move like ...Bf5?

Jamie: Not quite, but his move wasn't great either. He played **5...e5**?!

Jess: Why did you give it a ?!

Jamie: Because remember

when we discussed annotations in our first book, ?! represented a dubious move and I consider 5...e5 dubious!

Jess: It gets control of the centre, but doesn't

it just lose a pawn? Can't White just take the pawn on e5 for free?

Jamie: You tell me, Jess.

Jess: Well, that's what I'm going to do! **6. dxe5**, please.

Jamie: Correct – 2 points!

Jess: How silly of Black – just giving away a pawn like that!

Jamie: Well, Black hasn't actually lost a pawn. They can now get it back using a fork.

Jess: Oooh another tactic; let me find it!

Jamie: Waiting...

Jess: Don't rush me! I thought you said I should think about my moves?

Jamie: That's true, I'm sorry. Take your time.

Jess: I've got it now anyway! The pawn is undefended – that is the key! **6...Qa5+** will attack the pawn at the same time as delivering check and there is no way of defending both!

Jamie: That's not entirely true, Jess. 7. Qc3 would block the check and defend the pawn on e5.

Jess: But, that would then blunder the queen! Black could then just play 7...Bb4 and pin the queen! Bye bye, queen!

Jamie: How did you spot that move so quickly?

Jess: The pieces were on the same diagonal – it then makes it easy. I always look for pieces on the same ranks, files and diagonals for some cheeky tactics.

Jamie: Very impressive. Well, Reti is very smart and spotted that. He also considered his development to be more important than hanging onto that pawn.

Jess: Me too – it is the opening stage of the game. I will block the check. Either with 7. c3 or 7. Bd2.

Jamie: You need to pick one, Jess!

Jess: Argh, OK. Then 7. Bd2 because it actually develops a piece and then I can castle queenside on the next move.

Jamie: Correct again!

Jess: Woooop!

Jamie: Needless to say, Tartakower grabbed the 'free' pawn. **7...Qxe5**

Jess: Well, I already told you what I would do next – castle queenside!

Jamie: But you didn't look at the position! Don't just jump at an idea excitedly without analysing first!

Jess: Yes, you're right. OK, let me think. Argh – my knight is **en prise**! And it is pinned – oh gosh... must defend! OK, my move is 8. f3.

Jamie: Sorry Jess, Reti DID actually castle queenside! **8. O-O-O**

Jess: What? You tricked me!!

Jamie: Not really – you should have calculated.

Jess: But what about my knight?! I don't just want to give my opponent a free piece.

Jamie: Don't you think Reti thought of that? What do you think he had planned against that?

Jess: Ohhh I see it – If the queen takes the knight, I can play 9. Re1 and pin the queen against the king again! Pieces on the same file!

Jamie: Yup, exactly. The knight is **immune**.

Jess: Can't I have the points for that? I did get the right answer at first.

Jamie: But you changed your mind and you didn't see all the analysis.

Jess: I would have worked that out in a game if my opponent had taken my knight.

Jamie: It doesn't work like that – you need to have seen the moves BEFORE you make your decision. You can have 1 point though, as f3 does save your knight.

Jess: Thanks! Hang on a moment... I win the black queen if she takes the knight, but what if they use their knight on f6 to capture my knight? Don't I just lose the piece?!

Jamie: That is exactly what happened!
8...Nxe4

Jess: Oh nooooo! Now I've lost! I'm so stupid!

Jamie: Calm down, Jess, and just have a look at the position. You should never ever give up if you think you have made a mistake.

Jess: It's difficult – I am upset.

Jamie: I know, but when you get upset, it clouds your judgement, so try not to get upset and focus on what possibilities you have in this position.

Jess: OK, what about 9. Re1 anyway? I am pinning the knight again and so I can probably win it back?

Jamie: Yes, that move, followed by f3 at some point to put more pressure on the knight should win back the material lost. See – you did fine.

Jess: Is that what Reti played?

Jamie: Unfortunately not. Reti finished in explosive style.

Jess: Oh wow – tell me!

Jamie: Reti played 9. Qd8+!!!

Jess: No way! He just gave up his queen??

Jamie: He didn't give it up – he sacrificed it.

Jess: I would never have worked that out! OK, well Black's move is obvious – he has no choice but to take it. **9...Kxd8**

Jamie: So, how did he finish Tartakower off?

Jess: How about 10. Bf4? This is a discovered check and attacks the queen at the same time so I get back some of the material that is lost.

Jamie: That's true, but you have already sacrificed a rook AND a knight and after ...Qd5, you will lose another rook, so that is no good!

Jess: Hmmm, it definitely has something to do with a discovered check.

Jamie: Indeed it does. What is the special kind of discovered check you can do that ensures the defender has to move their king?

Jess: Ohhhh, a double check. That's what I will do. I have two to choose from – 10. Ba5+ and 10. Bg5+. Which one is it?

Jamie: That's for you to choose!

Jess: They both look like they lose the bishop, but that doesn't matter because it is also check from the rook, so the king has to move anyway. Hmmm, I am going to guess and say 10. Ba5+

Jamie: Sorry, Jess, the answer is **10. Bg5+**

Jess: Argh, it was a guess anyway. What difference does it make?

Jamie: If Reti had played 10. Ba5+, the black king would have gone to e7 and had the whole kingside to run away to. Reti cleverly cut down the number of squares that the king can run to by playing Bg5+. Now he only has two choices: 10...Kc7 and 10...Ke8.

Jess: I know what to do after both of these moves! I have been practising my mate in ones and I am very quick at these now!

Jamie: OK, so go ahead. How do you end Black's misery after each of the moves?

Jess: After 10...Ke8, the rook comes down to the back rank and checkmates with 11.Rd8# - another reason why the bishop is better on g5! Otherwise, e7 would not be covered.

Then after 10...Kc7, the bishop can come to d8 and checkmate the king, stopping it escaping via b6!

Jamie: Excellent work – those puzzles really did pay off!

Jess: Thanks, Jamie! That was such a good game and it really showed that development is very important in the beginning of the game.

Jamie: Not just in the beginning – having active pieces that are doing a lot and making threats is often much better than winning material. White is actually 12 points *down* in this final position, but they are the one with the victory!

Jess: How did I do overall, then?

Jamie: Very well! I was impressed by how much you played like a master! You got 16 points out of a possible 27.

Jess: Is that good?

Jamie: It's not bad! It means you still have room for improvement, but you did a good job!

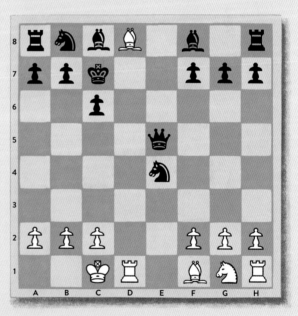

Jess: Great, thanks! Well I'm tired and need a rest now.

Jamie: You deserve it, Jess.

Bughouse

Harry: Hey, guys! You two have been working so ridiculously hard!

Jamie: Well, that's what you have to do if you want to become a chess grandmaster.

Marnie: You two definitely will if you keep this up!

Jess: I hope so, but we still have lots of work to do yet.

Harry: We came over because I thought you might want to have some fun after all your training.

Jess: I am definitely up for some fun.

Marnie: This will also help you practice your tactics and checkmating too.

Jamie: I definitely need some checkmating practice still!

Jess: Well, what is it?

Harry: It is a game called Bughouse.

Jess: Ewwww. I don't like bugs! I don't think I want to play!

Marnie: Neither do I, Jess. But don't worry, there are no bugs in the game!

Harry: It was actually called that because the game is so crazy and cool that it looks really random to someone who doesn't know what they are doing and they 'bug out' and go crazy.

Jamie: I hope that doesn't mean I will go crazy if I play!

Harry: Of course not. It is just a silly name, because the game is so fun!

Jess: As long as there are no actual bugs, I will play.

Marnie: I promise, Jess, otherwise I'm leaving with you!

Harry: There are no bugs, girls, and in order for this to work, all four of us need to play.

Jamie: Oh, cool, so is it like a team thing?

Harry: Yes, we play in pairs with two boards. It looks like two separate games are going on, but the cool thing is, when your partner takes a piece from their opponent, they can give it to you and you can then put it on your board as an extra piece.

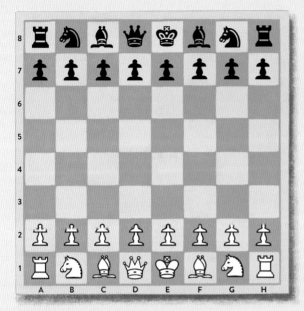

Jess: WOAH! That's so awesome!

Harry: I know! Therefore, you have to make sure you go the opposite colour to your opponent. So, let's set the boards up like this:

How about Marnie and I go on one team and you two go on the other team?

Jamie: Sounds good. So as soon as you get a piece, can you just place it down? Anywhere you like?

Harry: You have to wait your turn. It is just like a normal game of chess in that you take it in turns to make your move, only you get to make a move with a piece that isn't on the board.

Jess: So can I use my spare piece to take a piece?

Harry: No – no taking off with the piece. Just placing it down on the board.

Marnie: But you don't have to use the pieces straight away. You can save them for when a really good opportunity comes along. I save my knights until I can do a royal fork or something.

Jamie: Can you even put a piece down on a square when it gives check?

Marnie: Yeah! And checkmate!

Jess: No way! But that's so unfair if it is just suddenly checkmate.

Harry: Well, you can do it too! This is what is so difficult about this game. It is not about who has the most pieces, but who has the safer king. There will definitely be a lot of sacrificing in this game.

Jamie: Gosh, I'm scared. You know what I am like with checkmating.

Marnie: This is why it will be good practice for you.

Jamie: Isn't there an easier version?

Harry: Actually, there is. You can forbid putting down pieces in checkmate and pawns on the 7th rank, thereby making the game a little less complicated.

Jamie: That sounds much better! Can we play that version?

Jess: What about putting pawns on 8th ranks?

Harry: Jess, that would mean it could instantly promote! No, you can't do that, nor can you put them on the first rank. Yes, we can play the easier version first Jamie, but then we need to work our way up to the real Bughouse!

Marnie: Remember that the usual rules apply. If you are in check, you must get out of check immediately. You can use one of your spare pieces to block the check, however.

Harry: And also remember that when one board loses, your team loses!

Jess: Harsh! Can Jamie and I discuss what pieces we want?

Marnie: Sure, but no telling each other moves!

Jamie: No problem. Let's play!

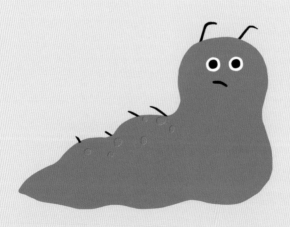

Goodbye

Jess: I can't believe we beat them!

Jamie: I know! It is amazing what hard work can do.

Jess: I am so happy!

Jamie: Well, I am exhausted and I think it is time for a rest.

Jess: I agree – it is well earned.

Jamie: I hope you all enjoyed our activity book and doing all the puzzles.

Jess: I know I did!

Jamie: If you manage to master all the puzzles in this book, you will be beating us in no time!

Jess: We need to keep practising then!

Jamie: Always.

Jess: Well, that's it from us for now. We hope to see you again soon!

Glossary

3-fold repetition: A type of draw. It occurs when the exact same position has occurred three times in the game. It does not have to be the same three moves in a row, but the same position.

50-move rule: A type of draw. It occurs when 50 moves for each side have been played, with no captures or pawn moves.

ABC of check: The three different ways to get out of check. A = Avoid, B = Block, C = Capture.

Absolute pin: A pin which absolutely stops a piece from moving. The piece is not allowed to move because it will be illegal.

Achilles' heel: The heel of a Greek hero. It is used to describe the f7 square in Black's starting line-up or the f2 square in White's starting line-up. It is a very weak spot in the army at the start of the game.

Advantageous exchange: An exchange of pieces from which one side gains material. It is advantageous to the side who gets the better pieces.

Attack: When one piece is in the line of fire of another piece. The piece can be attacked but not necessarily threatened (see threat).

Battery: More than one piece controlling the same rank, file or diagonal.

Bishop pair: When a player has two bishops and their opponent does not, there is a slight advantage for the bishop pair. Together, they have all the strengths of a bishop, but none of the weaknesses.

Box mate: The technique used when you are trying to checkmate a lone king with just a rook and a king. The idea is to cut the defending king's squares off, gradually, until he is trapped on the edge of the board.

Bull's head: An ideal opening structure. Following the three golden rules of the opening, this is the sort of position we would aim for because it controls the centre of the board and all our pieces are placed nicely for attack, while our king is safely castled.

Caro-Kann Defence: One of many chess openings that can be played. Tartakower played it in that famous game against Reti. It is a well-respected opening and leads to semi-open games.

Castling: The special move done with the king and rook in order to get the king safe. The rook and king do not swap places, but the king moves two squares and the rook jumps over.

Check: When the king is attacked. He must get out of check immediately.

Checkmate: When the king is trapped and the ABC of Check does not work. The king must be in check, or it is stalemate.

Closed game: A closed game/position is one where there is not so much room to move. There are usually lots of pawns on the board making it difficult for pieces to reach enemy territory. Closed games are usually quieter.

Complement: When two pieces work together well, they are said to complement each other.

Deflection: A type of the tactic in which an attack is made on a defender (see Removing the defender). Deflection is when you drive the defender away to another square where it can't do its defensive job anymore.

Diagonal: The angled straight line from one corner to another of the chessboard. It is along these that the bishops must travel.

Discovered attack/check: A discovered attack is when a player moves a piece out of the way to reveal an attack from another of their pieces that was behind it. A discovered check is the same principle, but the revealed piece is producing a check.

Double attack: When two pieces are being attacked at the same time. This is also known as a fork.

Double check: A double check can only occur from a discovered check. It is when a king is in check by two different pieces.

Doubled pawns: When two pawns of the same colour are situated on the same file. Doubled pawns are seen as weak because they make it difficult for each other to move.

Ending: The third stage of the game. Not many pieces are left on the board and the game will shortly come to an end.

En passant: A special move in which, when a pawn reaches the 5th rank, it may capture pawns in a different way – it can now capture a pawn that goes past it as if it has only moved one square.

En prise: A French phrase meaning that a piece is able to be taken for free. The literal translation means 'engaged'.

Etiquette: Good behaviour. You should behave in a certain way when playing chess.

Exchange: 1. To swap pieces of equal value. 2. The advantage of a rook for a knight or a bishop.

Family fork: An attack on a king, queen and rook at the same time.

File: The vertical rows of squares on the chessboard, named after letters.

Forced: This means the player has no choice but to play this move. These are the type of solutions you need to look for when doing Mate in Two puzzles. You have to make sure your opponent's reply is forced.

Fork: When one piece attacks more than one piece at the same time.

Immune: If a piece is immune, then it cannot be taken. There is usually something bad that will happen if that piece is taken, therefore it is immune from any threat.

Insufficient material: A type of draw. One side is left with not enough material to win the game. The other side will have just a king. The game will then be drawn.

Isolated pawn: A pawn that doesn't have any of its fellow pawns on the files either side of it is known as an isolated pawn. It is seen to be weak as it has no pawn to defend it and pawns are the best defenders.

Kingside: The four files on the right-hand side of the board – the side the king is on.

Kiss of death: The checkmate produced after the shadow technique is used, just using a queen and king.

Lawnmower: The checkmating technique using two rooks and a king versus a king. We call it 'Walking the Dog' in this book.

Line pieces: The pieces that control whole lines – the queen, the rooks and the bishops.

Material: Refers to pieces or points.

Middlegame: The second stage of the game. This is when most of the action occurs. It is the stage just after all of the pieces have been developed and when the two sides make plans.

Minor pieces: The knights and the bishops.

Notation: The moves of the game, written down to record them.

Open file: A file with no pawns at all on it is an open file.

Open game: An open game/position is one that has lots of space for the pieces to run around in. Usually, many pawns will have been traded and there are good attacking prospects for both sides. Open games are seen to be exciting.

Opening: The first stage of the game, in which the initial aim is to get the pieces out as quickly as possible and to castle.

Opposition: The situation in which both kings are opposite each other, one square apart. Whoever gains the opposition has the advantage. It is something used in endings.

Pin: Where a piece is pinned to a square and cannot move. There are two type of pin – see absolute pin and relative pin.

Promotion: When a pawn gets to the end of the board and can choose which piece it wants to turn into.

Queenside: The four files on the left-hand side of the board – the side where the queen is situated.

Rank: The horizontal lines going across the board, named after numbers.

Relative pin: A pin that doesn't completely stop a piece from being able to move, but discourages it from moving. The pinned piece in a relative pin can legally move, but usually won't want to for loss of material or worse.

Removing the defender: A very common tactic in games. There are several ways of trying to remove the defender, but if you have a plan and something is preventing it, get rid of that piece! You can capture the piece, deflect it, lure it away, etc.

Sacrifice: When you give up some material for a much higher gain. For example, if you give away your queen to ensure that you can checkmate your opponent.

Scholar's Mate: Also known as the four-move checkmate.

Semi-open file: A semi-open file is a file that has none of one side's pawns on it, but does have pawns or pieces of the other side.

Semi-open game: Just like we saw in the Reti-Tartakower game, openings such as the Caro-Kann Defence lead to semi-open positions. There is a reasonable amount of space, but perhaps only one of two sets of pawns have been traded. The Reti game became a lot more open after some more trades.

Skewer: Like a reverse pin, but where a more valuable piece is in front of a less valuable piece. When the more valuable piece moves to safety, the one behind can be captured.

Stalemate: Another type of draw, in which the player whose turn it is has no legal moves left and is not in check.

Strategy: The technique used in chess to help plan and make decisions.

Tactics: The tricks and traps used in chess to try to win material.

Threat: When there is an attack that can be executed on the next go. A threat is something that should be dealt with immediately.

Touch move/take: A tournament rule – if you touch a piece, you must move it. Likewise, if you touch one of your opponent's pieces, you must take it if you can.

Under promotion: When a pawn gets to the end of the board and promotes to any other piece than a queen.

Variant: Any variation of the game of chess that doesn't have the standard rules.

Visualization: The process of calculating moves in your head, without moving the pieces.

X-ray: Also known as a skewer.

INDEX

ABC of check 49, 110
absolute pin 78, 110, 112
Achilles' heel 110
advantageous exchange 110
attack 23, 83, 110, 111

battery 110
bingo, co-ordinate 44–7
bishops 16–19, 40, 71
  bishop pair 110
  knights vs. bishops 36–9
  pins, forks and skewers 77–8
  points 63
box 'em in challenge 94–5
box mate 110
bughouse 106–8
bull's head 110

capture 41
  giveaway chess 68–9
  good and bad capture 66–7
Caro-Kann Defence 97, 110, 113
castling 32, 41, 73, 110
check 41, 48–9, 82, 83, 110, 111
  ABC of 49, 110
  three check chess 54–5
checkmate 41, 48–9, 110, 113
  box 'em in challenge 94–5
  checkmate challenge 50–1
  kiss of death 92, 112
  mate in one puzzle 52–3
  mate in two puzzle 58–9
  shadow mate challenge 92–3
  walking the dog challenge 90–1, 112
chessboards, 9x9 29
closed game 111
closed positions 97, 111
complement 111
co-ordinate bingo 44–7
cops and robbers strategy 17, 18–19

deflection 111
diagonal 111
discovered attack 82, 83, 86, 100, 111
discovered check 41, 82, 83, 86, 104, 111

double attack 19, 111
double check 41, 83, 104, 111
doubled pawns 99, 111
draws 110

en passant 9, 10–11, 111
en prise 102, 111
ending 111
etiquette 111
exchange 66, 111

family fork 111
50-move rule 110
file 111, 112
forced checkmate 58–9, 111
forks 19, 76–7, 80–1, 111
4-move checkmate 113

giveaway chess 68–9
guess the move 96–105

hungry horse strategy 21, 22–3

immune 103, 111
insufficient material 112
isolated pawn 35, 112

Jesön Mor 28–9

kings 10, 30–3, 69
  box 'em in challenge 94–5
  check and checkmate 48–55, 83–4, 110, 111, 112
  mine alert! 31–3
  notation 40, 41
  pins 78
kingside 112
kiss of death 92, 112
knights 20–9, 40, 41, 71–2
  forks 76–7
  hungry horse strategy 21, 22–3
  Jesön Mor 28–9
  knight's tour 24–5, 26

knights vs. bishops 36–9
  points 63

lawnmower (walking the dog) 90–1, 112
line pieces 16–19, 77–8, 112

mate in one puzzle 52–3
mate in two puzzle 58–9, 111
material 112
maths 64–5
middlegame 112
mine alert! 31, 32–3
minor pieces 71, 112

9x9 chessboard 29
notation 40–4, 112

open file 35, 112
open game 112
open positions 97, 112
opening principles 70–3, 97, 112
opposition 112

pawns 8–11, 40, 73, 112, 113
  cops and robbers 17, 18–19
  doubled pawns 99, 111
  en passant 9, 10–11, 111
  isolated pawns 35, 112
  pawn wars strategy 11, 12–15
  promotion 9–10
pins 76, 78, 80–1, 110, 112
points, scoring 62–5
progressive chess 60–1
promotion 9–10, 112
puzzles
  mate in one puzzle 52–3
  mate in two puzzle 58–9, 111
  yes, no or maybe puzzle 74–5

queens 10, 16–19, 73, 113
  cops and robbers strategy 17, 18–19
  notation 40
  pins 77–8
  queenside 112
  shadow mate challenge 92–3

rank 113
relative pin 78, 100, 112, 113

removing the defender 84–6, 111, 113
Reti, Richard 96–105, 110, 113
rooks 16–19, 40, 77–8
  box 'em in challenge 94–5
  walking the dog challenge 90–1, 112

sacrifice 14, 55, 85, 103, 104, 113
Scholar's Mate 42, 113
scoring points 62–5
semi-open file 35, 113
semi-open game 113
semi-open positions 97, 113
shadow mate challenge 92–3
skewers 19, 77, 79, 80–1, 113
SPAF 80–1
stalemate 48, 93, 94, 110, 113
strategy 113
  cops and robbers strategy 17, 18–19
  hungry horse strategy 21, 22–3
  introduction to 34–9
  knights vs. bishops 36–9
  opening principles 70–3
  pawn wars 11, 12–15

tactics 76–89, 100, 113
  SPAF 80–1
  spot the tactic 86–7
Tartakower, Saviely 96–105, 110, 113
thinking ahead 56–7
threats 113
  spotting and stopping 88–9
three check chess 54–5
3-fold repetition 110
touch move 56–8, 60, 113

under-promotion 113

variants of chess 26–7, 113
visualization 56–7, 113
  progressive chess 60–1

walking the dog challenge 90–1, 112

x-ray 79, 113

ANSWERS TO PUZZLES

Mine Alert: page 32

Jamie: How did you get on with these, Jess?

Jess: Pretty well; sometimes I didn't always choose the quickest route, but at least I didn't step on any mines!

Puzzle 1

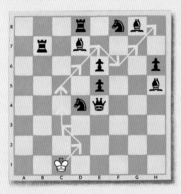

Puzzle 2

Puzzle 3

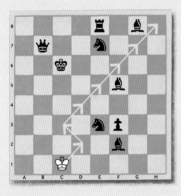

Puzzle 4

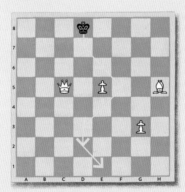

Mate in One: page 52

Puzzle 1: Starting off with an easy one, you just need to remember to put your queen as close as possible to the enemy king, where it is safe.
Answer: Qc7#.

Puzzle 2: Despite being an endgame, the black king is in grave danger as it has run out of squares. The combination of the knight and rook and king is deadly.
Answer: Re6#.

Puzzle 3: A very pretty checkmate; a discovered checkmate if you like! White makes use of their long-range pieces by moving their pawn out of the way to clear the path for the bishop, while simultaneously covering the f5 square.
Answer: g4#.

Puzzle 4: It is clear that White is winning here, but it looks like Black can be checkmated in numerous ways. However, moves like Qc4+ fail as Black has escape squares. There is only one mate in one.
Answer: Qd7#.

Puzzle 5: Another discovered checkmate! It is easy to see that if you move the rook on d4 out of the way, the black king will be in check. The difficult part is working out which square to go to. Instinctively, most will say d7 as it covers g7 and is on a nice attacking square. However, it does not cover g8. There is a better square and it is irrelevant that it is 'not safe' as Black is in check!
Answer: Rxg4#.

Puzzle 6: Again, Black's king is in serious danger and it looks like moves such as Qb3 will checkmate. However, Black has a sneaky escape square on b5, so this must be covered at the same time. Yet another discovered checkmate.
Answer: c4#.

Mate in Two: page 58

Puzzle 1: Somewhat a trick question as there is indeed a mate in two: 1. Rxd8+ Kxd8 2. Qxd7#. However, there is actually a mate in one due to the fact the rook on d8 is pinned!

Answer: Qxd7 is instantly mate, but Rxd8+ followed by Qxd7 is also correct for a mate in two.

Puzzle 2: What a crazy position! There is a rook on e8 that can be taken for free, while getting a free queen in the process! However, then Black can take on f1 with check and it is all very complicated. White must maintain the initiative.

Answer: 1. Ne6+; If ...Rxe6, then f8=Q#. If ...Kh8, then fxe8=Q# White has two choices to finish Black off!

Puzzle 3: This position is rather pretty – Black has a queen, but White has more pieces and they are more dangerously placed around Black's queen. White can sacrifice to finish off the game, despite being material down at the end.

Answer: 1. Rd8+ Qxd8 2. Ng6#.

Puzzle 4: In all of these positions, the attacker is very close to checkmating immediately, but there is something in the way. Usually you must remove that defender and then you are free to continue with your plan. Here, the bishop defends against both Ng3+ and Rg5+, but it is overworked.

Answer: 1. Ng3+ Bxg3 2. Rg5#.

Puzzle 5: If you got the answer to this one, that is most impressive! This is exceptionally difficult and revolves around the idea of a zugzwang; where every possible move is a bad one!

Answer: 1. Qd6!! is the only mate in two. Now, if the rook moves, 2. Qxd7 is checkmate. If the c-pawn moves to c6 or c5, then 2. Qb8 is checkmate, and if 1...cxd6, then 2. Rc1#.

Puzzle 6: Something has gone terribly wrong for Black to have their king on c6 so early in the game! It is inevitable that any check will eventually lead to a checkmate! Therefore, it is no surprise that there is a queen sacrifice that leads to checkmate in 2 moves. White's pieces are simply too powerful.

Answer: 1. Qd5+ Nxd5 2. exd5#.

Chess Maths: page 64

1. $5 + 3 + 3 + 3 = 14$
2. $(9 + 6) \div 3 = 15 \div 3 = 5$
3. $(10 + 3 + 1) \div 2 = 14 \div 2 = 7$
4. $(9 + 1) \times (5 + 3) = 10 \times 8 = 80$
5. Trick question as the king has no points value! $(3 \times 3) + 0 = 9$.

Good Capture/Bad Capture: page 66

Puzzle 1:

White:

1. Bxa5 = Good Capture
White will gain 9 points, but lose 3, therefore gaining 6 points overall

2. Bxb5 = Bad Capture
White will gain 1 point, but lose 3, therefore losing 2 points overall

3. Nxc7 = Bad Capture
White will gain 1 point, but lose 3, therefore losing 2 points overall

4. Nxf6 = Exchange
White will gain 3 points, but lose 3, therefore making it an equal trade

5. Nxf7 = Good Capture
White will gain 1 point and not lose anything as it is defended by the queen, therefore gaining 1 point overall

6. Nxh7 = Bad Capture
White will gain 1 point and lose 3, therefore losing 2 points overall

7. Qxf7+ = Good Capture
White will gain 1 point and not lose anything as it is defended by the knight, therefore gaining 1 point overall

8. Qxh7+ = Bad Capture
White will gain 1 point and lose 9, therefore losing 8 points overall.

Black:

1. Qxa2 = Bad Capture
Black will gain 1 point, but lose 9 points, therefore losing 8 points overall

2. Qxd2 = Good Capture
Black will gain 3 points and not lose anything as the bishop is undefended, therefore gaining 3 points overall

3. Bxc4 = Good Capture
Black will gain 3 points and lose 1, therefore gaining 2 points overall

4. Bxf2+ = Bad Capture
Black will gain 1 point and lose 3, therefore losing 2 overall

5. Bxh3 = Good Capture
Black will gain 5 points and lose 3, therefore gaining 2 overall

6. Nxd5 = Exchange
Black will gain 3 points, but lose 3, therefore making it an equal trade

7. Nxe4 = Bad Capture
Black will gain 1 point, but lose 3, therefore losing 2 overall

8. Nxh5 = Good Capture
Black will gain 9 points, but lose 3, therefore gaining 6 points overall.

Puzzle Two:

White:

1. Bxc6 = Exchange
White will gain 3 points, but lose 3, therefore making it an equal trade
2. Nxa5 = Exchange
White will gain 3 points, but lose 3, therefore making it an equal trade
3. Nxc5 = Bad Capture
White will gain 1 point and lose 3, therefore losing 2 points overall
4. Nxd4 = Good Capture
White will gain 5 points and lose 3, therefore gaining 2 overall
5. Rxc5 = Bad Capture
White will gain 1 point and lose 5, therefore losing 4 points overall
6. Qxh5 = Good Capture
White will gain 9 points and not lose anything as it is undefended, therefore gaining 9 points overall
7. Bxd4 = Good Capture
White will gain 5 points and lose 3, therefore gaining 2 overall
8. exd6+ = Exchange
White will gain 1 point, but lose 1, therefore making it an equal trade
9. Rxg7 = Good Capture
White will gain 1 point and not lose anything as it is undefended, therefore gaining 1 point overall.

Black:

1. Bxd2 = Bad Capture
Black will gain 1 point, but lose 3, therefore losing 2 overall
2. Rxa4 = Good Capture
Black will gain 3 points and not lose anything as it is undefended, therefore gaining 3 points overall
3. Nxe5 = Good Capture
Black will gain 1 point and not lose anything as it is undefended, therefore gaining 1 point overall
4. Rxd2 = Bad Capture
Black will gain 1 point, but lose 5, therefore losing 4 overall
5. Qxd1 = Exchange
Black will gain 9 points, but lose 9, therefore making it an equal trade
6. Qxh2+ = Bad Capture
Black will gain 1 point, but lose 9, therefore losing 8 points overall.

Yes, No or Maybe: page 74

Puzzle 1:
A) Nf3 = Yes. Developing a piece towards the centre is good.
B) Na3 = No. Knights on the rim are dim.
C) Bb5 = Maybe. I am not sure where is best for the bishop at the moment and I would rather develop my knights first, but the move is OK and it is developing.

Puzzle 2:
A) Nc3: Yes. Developing a piece towards the centre while defending e4.
B) Bc4: No. While this is a good developing move, it leaves the pawn on e4 undefended.
C) Bb5+: Maybe. It is developing and may seem like a good move as you are checking the opponent's king, but after ...c6, you will have to run straight back again.

Puzzle 3:
A) Bg5: Yes. Developing and making a relative pin.
B) h3: Maybe. Doesn't really help your development, but the move doesn't harm you.
C) c5: Maybe. Again, doesn't help development and also releases tension in the centre, but it doesn't blunder.

Puzzle 4:
A) Qh4: No. Do not bring your queen out too early!
B) Nh6: No. Knights on the rim are dim!
C) d5: No. This move just gives away a pawn! A sensible move in this position would be any developing move like 2... Nf6.

Spot the Tactic: page 86

Puzzle 1: A classic removing the defender position. Black wants to take the bishop on g5, but cannot at the moment because it is defended by the knight on f3. Therefore, Black removes this defender and is free to capture the bishop on the next go!
Answer: 1...Bxf3 2. Qxf3 Qxg5.

Puzzle 2: Another removing the defender, but Black is driving the white king away. It is the only piece defending the rook on d5.
Answer: 1...Bb6+ and any king move leads to 2...Rxe4. If White tries to defend and block the check with Nc5, then after 2...Bxc5+3. Kxc5, the rook is undefended again.

Puzzle 3: The only defender of the knight on e5 is the bishop on d6. If that bishop gets pushed away...
Answer: 1. c5 followed by 2. Bxe5.

Puzzle 4: Tactics often come from undefended pieces! The black bishop on g4 is begging to be attacked! It must be done by a discovered attack.
Answer: 1. dxc5 and now both the bishop on d6 and the bishop on g4 are attacked and one of them must drop.

Puzzle 5: In addition to the undefended pieces, if you look out for pieces on the same ranks, files and diagonals, you will often find some kind of tactic. This time it is a classic discovered attack.
Answer: 1...Bh2+ and no matter what White does, Black can play 2...Qxb7.

Puzzle 6: A tricky question, but it comes from the fact that the white queen is overworked. It is trying to defend the knight on b5 and the rook on a2 at the same time. There are two solutions.
Answer 1: 1...Rxb5 and if the queen

captures, then Black can capture the rook on a2 and be a piece up.

Answer 2: 1...Bd3! This is a very clever move, forking the queen and knight. If the queen captures for 'free', then the rook on a2 can still be captured.

Spot the Threat, Stop the Threat: page 88

Puzzle 1: White is threatening a checkmate on g7 and h8, so it is difficult to stop both of them at the same time. The reason why the threat is there is because of the strong battery between the queen and bishop down that diagonal. If the connection between them is blocked, the threat is no longer there.

Answer: 1...Ne5.

Puzzle 2: Black is threatening Qa1#. However, White cannot defend the square, nor block the path to a1, so the options are limited. The only choice is to run! Luckily, White is already up on material and can hide safely on d2.

Answer: Kc1!

Puzzle 3: Attack is the best form of defence. There is a lot going on here and Black has a knight on f4 that is being attacked, but White's king is in trouble. Therefore, Black should strike while the iron is hot.

Answer: 1...Qg2+ 2. Qxg2 fxg2#.

Puzzle 4: Black is threatening checkmate on b2, but White has an attacking position. Can he get in there first with a checkmate? We must only analyze forcing moves as it is checkmate next move. Rxg6+ fxg6, Qxg6+ looks tempting, but after Kh8, White has nothing. Therefore, it is better to just defend rather than losing the material.

Answer: 1. Bc1.

Puzzle 5: Strange to have to spot the threat when Black is already forking White's rooks. However, this is all about trying to find a way out of it. The answer seems a little bit counter-intuitive but it is clever.

Answer: 1. Bxc4! Nxc4 and the rooks are forked again. However, after 2. Rh2+, White will then have a spare move to get the other rook to safety after Black deals with the check.

Puzzle 6: Another checkmate is threatened on b2, but this time White IS quicker. White can play a fantastic sacrificial combination to deliver a forced mate in three.

Answer: 1. Rh8+ Kxh8 2. Qh6+ and the queen cannot be captured due to the pawn on g7 being pinned. After Kg8, 3. Qxg7 is checkmate.

Guess the Move: page 96

Move 2:
d4 .... 2 points
Nf3, Nc3, d3 .... 1 point

Move 3:
Nc3 .... 2 points
e5, exd5, Nd2 .... 2 points
Bd3, f3 .... 1 point

Move 4:
Nxe4 .... 1 point

Move 5:
Qd3 .... 3 points
Nxf6+, Ng3, Nc3, Bd3 .... 2 points

Move 6:
dxe5 .... 2 points

Move 7:
Bd2 .... 3 points
Nc3, Nd2 .... 2 points

Move 8:
0-0-0 .... 3 points
f3 .... 1 point

Move 9:
Qd8+ .... 5 points
Re1 .... 2 points

Move 10:
Bg5+ .... 3 points
Bf4+, Bc3+ .... 1 point

Move 11:
Bd8# and Rd8# .... 3 points

Maximum: .... 27 points.